# A History of Quidi Vidi

## By Jean Edwards Stacey

DRC Publishing
St. John's

First edition published by DRC Publishing 2002

DRC Publishing
3 Parliament Street
St. John's, Newfoundland
A1A 2Y6
(709) 726-0960

e-mail: staceypj@avint.net

National Library of Canada Cataloguing in Publication

Stacey, Jean Edwards

A History of Quidi Vidi / Jean Edwards Stacey

Canadian Cataloging in Publication Data

Stacey, Jean Edwards

A History of Quid Vidi

Includes bibliographical references.

ISBN 0-9684209-3-1

1. Quidi Vidi (St. John's, Nfld.)—History. I. Title.

FC2196.52.S73 2002 971.8'1 C2002-902535-4

F1124.5.S14S73 2002


Composition, design, covers: Ken Simmons, FineTuneIt@netscape.net
Front cover: Quidi Vidi, a photograph taken by Peter Stacey
Back Cover: Postcard of Quidi Vidi

# Table of Contents

# Introduction to Quidi Vidi

*I*n the early morning of a winter's day, the village of Quidi Vidi lies hushed and silent under a blanket of snow, the sky is grey with a promise of yet more snow to come, and the grey of the sky is reflected in the harbour water.

**Quidi Vidi in winter.**

By Peter Stacey

In Quidi Vidi, the narrow inlet to the harbour is known as the "Gut" and acts as a shelter for fishing boats from the stormy Atlantic just outside. On this particular winter's day, the Gut is deserted, as is the narrow winding road which meanders through the village. There are houses all around but not a person to be seen.

Standing by the side of the road looking at houses backed by rocky cliffs and gazing out the harbour towards the ocean, you could be forgiven for thinking you are alone in the universe, but you are, in fact, in a part of the City of St. John's, provincial capital of Newfoundland and Labrador.

Quidi Vidi village is in the eastern periphery of the city, and it's difficult to believe you can simply turn a corner and be in a place which is so un-citylike, and continues to have its own very special character and charm.

In tourist brochures, Quidi Vidi is described as a 17th-century fishing village which lies within city limits at the base of Signal Hill. Picturesque, quaint and unique are adjectives often used to describe the settlement situated between Quidi Vidi Lake, which is the site of the famed Royal St. John's Regatta, and Quidi Vidi Gut.

First inhabited in the early 16th century, Quidi Vidi village is appealing in winter, but it is in summer — when the air is warm and scented with the sharp tang of salt water, when small fishing boats bob in the Gut, when boats overturned on a wooden wharf are draped with fishing nets, when seagulls swoop and soar from the high granite cliffs encircling the harbour — that tourists come in flocks.

In summer, Quidi Vidi is likely one of the most photographed places in all of Newfoundland.

# Quidi Vidi or Titti Whitti?

*S*ome of the name Quidi Vidi has been referred to over the years include: Quiteandy; Quilliwiddi, Kitte Vitte; Kerividi; Quimidity; Quirividy; Qity Vety; Quiddibiddy, Quide Vide, Cety Vety and Queue de Vide.

In 1794, British seaman Aaron Thomas provided a unique variation of the name when he noted in his journal: "You must know that there is a singular place about two miles from St. John's called Titti Whitti."

The spelling Quidi Vidi first appeared in 1708, while the name Quiddy Viddy showed up in a 1780 British administrative document.

No one has a definitive answer as to just where the name Quidi Vidi originated.

There are numerous theories and much speculation but apparently no one right answer.

Some people claim the village is named after a lady named Kitty Vitty who once ran a tavern there. Others say the name came from Qui Divida, a reference to the opening in the wall of rock that leads from the village to the sea. Someone else has a theory that an early ship's captain used Latin to keep the daily log and Quidi Vidi translates simply to mean "the place that we saw."

There is speculation too that the names quidimiti and Quimiditi, found in French documents of 1704, suggest a Beothuck origin.

In his book, Place Names of the Avalon Peninsula, Dr. Ronald Seary suggests that Quidi Vidi might well be derived from a French family name which occurs as Quedville in both Normandy and Picardy, as Quidiville in Picardy, Quiedeville in Normandy, and as Quetteville in Jersey.

Seary says the name could as well be from the French place name, Quetteville, near Honfleur.

The community today is called Quidi Vidi and the three accepted pronunciation are: Kitty Vitty, Kiddy Viddy and Kwida Vida. Some people, including residents of Quidi Vidi, get around the pronunciation issue by simply referring to the community as "The Gut" or "The Village."

Early mention of Quidi Vidi village dates from 1669 when James Yonge, a surgeon with the Devon fishing fleet in St. John's, wrote in his journal that he had been once to Petty Harbour and twice to a place he called Kitty-vitty.

In 1762, British and French troops fought a battle near Quidi Vidi. This was after the British landed at Torbay and marched overland to recapture St. John's from the French. The battle began at Quidi Vidi Pass Battery, a site marked today by a plaque located on a hill just above Coronation Bridge on the south end of Quidi Vidi Lake. In 1782, the British fortified the hill with two six-pound

**Quidi Vidi Battery**

By Peter Stacey

cannons and entrenchments for 100 soldiers. The military abandoned the hill in 1824 and the artillery was removed.

Another steep hill, this one overlooking the entrance to Quidi Vidi Harbour, has long been part of the outer defenses of St. John's and it is here that Quidi Vidi Battery is located.

When the French invaded St. John's in 1762, they recognized the importance of this very significant spot and fortified it with two cannons and a detachment of soldiers. The British succeeded in captured the battery on September 14, 1762. Under British control, Quidi Vidi Battery deteriorated until the outbreak of the American Revolution, when it was reinforced with six pieces of artillery in anticipation of raids by American privateers. When peace was declared, the battery again fell into ruin. It was reactivated during the Napoleonic Wars and equipped with four 18-pound cannon and three six-pound cannon. In 1812, during Great Britain's war with the United States, a guard house, powder magazine and four artillery pieces were placed at the battery and it was garrisoned by a body of soldiers, supplemented by local volunteers.

Following the end of that war, one or two men were stationed there until all British troops were withdrawn from Newfoundland in 1870. Now reconstructed to the 1812 period, Quidi Vidi Battery is open to the public in season.

3

# A New Found Land

*B*y the year 1610, Great Britain had established colonies in British America as far south as Virginia, and that year a Royal Charter was issued to the London and Bristol Company to set up a colony in Newfoundland, a wild land in the New World, which Sir Humphrey Gilbert had claimed in the name of Queen Elizabeth in 1583.

Newfoundland was where Venetian John Cabot had landed and planted a flag in the name of King Henry VII on June 24, 1497, thus giving England a foothold in the New World and laying the foundation for her Colonial Empire. Stretching far out into the North Atlantic, the nearest part of North America to Europe, Newfoundland's appeal for the English and foreign fisherman who frequented its shores were the offshore waters that teemed with codfish.

In England's West Country there were many merchants and shipowners who realized they could make good profits by sending fishing ships to Newfoundland. Every year they sent out more than 100 ships, which arrived in June and began fishing as soon as weather and ice conditions would allow. The fishermen on these boats built stages, wharves, flakes and stores. In the fall, when the fish had been dried, they loaded it into their boats and carried it back to sell in England, France, Spain and Portugal.

There were many people in England who thought that the fishermen would do better to live in Newfoundland all the year round. This would enable them to build their boats, stages and flakes, cut their firewood and prepare their fishing equipment during the winter. They would be able to begin fishing early in the spring and, because they would not have to return to England in the fall, could continue to fish longer each year.

As well, those who settled in Newfoundland would be able to prevent French, Spanish and Portuguese fishermen from fishing in Newfoundland waters, ensuring English fishermen controlled the whole of the Newfoundland fishery. However, merchants from England's West Country — some call them Western Adventurers — had their own reasons for not wanting settlers in Newfoundland. The merchants knew that settlers would take the best fishing places, the best harbours and the best sites for their flakes and stages. The merchants' view of settlement was that it would no longer entitle them to sole access of the rich fishing grounds off of Newfoundland.

The British government's method of dealing with the thorny issue of settlement was to allow merchants from London and Bristol to start a colony in Newfoundland while, at the same time, ordering them not to interfere with the English fishermen who came in the summer.

# Cuper's Cove

*T*he basic land grant given to the merchants of London and Bristol in 1610 comprised the whole of the Avalon Peninsula, the shores of Trinity Bay and the Bonavista Peninsula.

In August 1610, 39 colonists led by Bristol merchant John Guy arrived at Cupids, what they called Cuper's Cove, in Conception Bay. Here, they established the first English settlement in what is now Canada. Cupids is also one of the earliest European settlements anywhere in North America.

*The James Cook & Michael Lane Map, 1775*
*National Map Collection, National Archives of Canada #52302*

By 1613, the population of Cuper's Cove had increased to 62, including a baby boy born to settler Nicholas Guy and his wife on March 27, 1613. The baby was the first English child born in Canada.

Offshoots of Guy's colony were later established in nearby Bristol's Hope and Harbour Grace. Colonies were established as well in Renews by Sir William Vaughan and in Ferryland by Sir George Calvert, later Lord Baltimore. According to Judge Daniel Prowse in his 1895 History of Newfoundland, there was as well a distinct colony of St. John's which extended south from Cape St. Francis to Petty Harbour and out as far as Holyrood.

In 1625, King Charles I granted an exclusive monopoly of the island to West Country fishermen.

Eight years later, in 1633, he followed through with the Star Chamber Rules, his infamous code of regulations for the governance of the fishery. Among the most noteworthy provisions of the Star Chamber Rules were, forbidding owners of fishing ships to bring anyone to Newfoundland who intended to settle there and establishing rule by fishing admirals.

Under the fishing admiral system, as recognized by law, the captain of the first ship to arrive in any harbour in the spring became admiral of the harbour for that year. The second arrival became vice-admiral, the third rear admiral. These so called admirals had power to take all the best fishing premises for their own men. During the fishing season, they functioned as governor, parliament and law court.

# The 1600s

*F*ishermen from Spain, Portugal and France fished on the Grand Banks of Newfoundland then salted their catch of codfish on board their vessels and brought it back to Europe to be dried and sold.

English fishermen, not having as ready access to the supplies of salt available to Spanish, Portuguese and French fishermen, developed a system which involved light salting for a short period followed by thorough washing and then drying in the open air on wooden flakes. The process of salting and drying fish is referred to in Newfoundland as "making fish."

Most of the English fished inshore, fishing daily from small boats with hook and line, using sea birds, herring, capelin and squid as bait, and returning to shore each evening. They set up operation on sites close to the fishing grounds and built stages for splitting and salting fish, flakes on which the codfish were laid to dry, and cook rooms and bunk houses for the crews. These fishing sites or rooms eventually became settlements extending all around the island and along the coast of Labrador.

In the 1600s, there were approximately 1,000 permanent residents scattered in villages along the Newfoundland coast. There was as well a fluctuating body of about 1,500 bye-boat keepers and their servants. Bye-boatmen were individuals financed by merchants to come to Newfoundland as passengers on trading vessels. Once here, they hired small vessels and cheap labour to catch fish for the export market. Many of the bye-boatmen ended up settling in Newfoundland.

The servants were fishing servants, or hired fishermen, often young Irishmen who came over with bye-boatmen or arrived on one of the West Country vessels that regularly stopped to get provisioned in the Irish ports of Waterford and Cork.

Fishing servants came as well from England's West Country, as noted by Prowse on page 297 of his history:

*The Late Hon. Stephen Rendell has often told me that even when he came to the Colony in 1834, hundreds of sturdy Devonshire lads came out every spring to Rowell's, Boden's, Bulley's, Mudge's, Job's, and many others on the South Side and in Hoyle's Town (Maggoty Cove) and to Torbay, Bay Bulls, Petty Harbour and etc. All these "youngsters" were shipped for two summers and a winter.*

*Mr. Rendell said nearly every labouring man about Coffinswell had been a servant in Newfoundland. The regular place for shipping was at Newtown Abbott, in the still existing hostelry, "The Dartmouth Inn and Newfoundland Tavern." Here the engagement* was *"wetted"* with cyder, strong beer, and the still more potent Jamaica. There were the same scenes enacted every spring. The coming and going of the Newfoundland men was an event in Devonshire. The rurals reckoned the time by the old Church of England lectionary: *"Jan! The Parson be in Pruverbs, the Newfanlan men will soon be a coming whome."*

In 1638, with the early land patents expired, Sir David Kirke succeeded in obtaining a patent for all of Newfoundland. Kirke arrived with his wife and children and 100 men. He took possession of the stone mansion Lord Baltimore had built in Ferryland and immediately set to work to make money, charging rent for stage rooms, selling tavern licenses, and making every foreigner pay him a commission of five fish for every 120 fish caught.

**Flakes and stage at the Gut**

Collection of Peg Magnone

Kirke was recalled to England in 1640, following complaints that he was withholding taxes from his London partners. He was replaced as governor by John Downing, a London merchant, whose instructions included to live in the house in Ferryland and to civilize the Indians living in Newfoundland so that, in time, they would be brought to know God.

In 1642, a rebellious English Parliament fielded armies that marched against King Charles and his loyal peers. The supporters of Parliament, called Roundheads, were led by Oliver Cromwell and they eventually triumphed over the king's supporters, who were known as Cavaliers or Royalists.

On January 30, 1649, in the immediate wake of England's civil war, Charles I was beheaded and Cromwell took his place as chief of state. What followed was known as the Commonwealth Period, during which time commissioners were appointed to govern Newfoundland. The most distinguished of these commissioners was John Treworgie, who managed the colony from 1653 to 1660. During his administration, Treworgie didn't permit settlers to be treated unjustly. He encouraged land cultivation and promoted trade between Newfoundland and the continental colonies. Prowse refers to Treworgie's seven-year administration as the one bright spot amidst a dreary record of wrong and oppression.

# Attempted Expulsion of Settlers

*B*y the end of the Commonwealth period, trade between Newfoundland and New England was firmly established. The New Englanders, who were mostly traders and not fishermen, bought inferior fish English merchants didn't want and sold it for a profit in the English West India Islands.

They also sold provisions to Newfoundland settlers, everything from cattle and corn to lumber, and did a thriving trade in rum, selling it for 25 cents a gallon wholesale. In 1789, wily Newfoundland merchants were retailing rum to fishermen for a profitable $1.25 a gallon.

Following the death of Cromwell and the accession of his son, Richard, as Lord Protector, the demand for restoration of the royalty increased.

Charles II, son of Charles I, was crowned king in 1661. It is Prowse's contention the two most important events that occurred in Newfoundland during Charles II's reign were the French founding a colony in Placentia in 1662 with the king's blessing, and the attempted expulsion of settlers by an Order in Council from the monarch in 1675.

Sir Josiah Child, leader of England's powerful West Country merchants, was largely responsible for the move to try and expel settlers from Newfoundland. In 1670, Child wrote a pamphlet expressing fear that settlements in Newfoundland were prejudicial to the migratory summer fishery and to the national interest.

He argued the fishery is the recognized training ground for a country's navy and this training ground would be destroyed if the shore fishery were allowed to increase at the expense of the bank fishery. Already, he said, sailing ships involved in the fishery had decreased from 250 to 80.

Furthermore, said Child, merchants in England were losing out on business because most of the provisions the Newfoundland settlers used, including bread, beef, pork, butter, cheese, clothes, linen and wool, as well as fishing nets and lines, were supplied from either Ireland or New England.

On January 27, 1675, King Charles II, largely influenced by Child's writings, reaffirmed and added to the Star Chamber Rules his father had issued in 1633. His additions included prohibiting settlement within six miles of the shore, giving summer fishermen first choice of the best fishing places and requiring masters of all vessels to post a bond of £100 to ensure anyone brought out to Newfoundland was returned to England.

In what was a final act of insult, Commodore Sir John Berry was given orders to go to Newfoundland, burn houses, and move all settlers back to England or make them go to the West Indies.

Berry, who had earlier been a West Country fisherman and

whose brother was in the fish trade, was sympathetic to the settlers' plight. On arrival, his first act was to sail along the coast, counting inhabitants and talking to them.

In 1675, Newfoundland was home to approximately 1,200 settlers, with the four principal settlements being St. John's, Ferryland, Harbour Grace and Quidi Vidi. A 1676 report of English inhabitants of Newfoundland listed the residents of "Quide Vide" as a widow named Wood who had one child, owned one boat and employed four fishing servants, and a single man by the name of Richard England who, like the widow, owned one boat and employed four fishing servants.

Berry quickly found out the settlers didn't want to leave their homes and that many had lived in Newfoundland for years. Merchant Thomas Oxford, for example, reported he and his family had lived in St. John's for about 70 years. Over the years, the settlers had raised families, cleared land and built houses, barns and fishing stages. They had planted gardens where they grew vegetables, and cultivated apple trees and small bushes which had been brought from the old country and endured to blossom and bear fruit.

In spite of hardships, which included attacks by pirates and fears of invasion by enemies such as the French and Dutch, the settlers wanted to stay. They had made many efforts to have England appoint a governor for Newfoundland. Among those who had expressed interested in the position were Captain Robert Robinson, William Hinton and William Downing, a son of John Downing who had been sent out to Newfoundland to take the place of Sir David Kirke in 1640. As part of his bid to be governor, Downing had proposed a tax on fishing boats and knew just the man best to collect it: his brother, "Mr. John Downing at Que de Vide," as well as "George Kirke Esquire at Fermouze; Mr. Thomas Oxford, St. John's; and Mr. John Pinn at Havre de Grace."

Prowse compares the situation in which the Newfoundland settlers found themselves in 1675 as akin to the French Acadians who were driven out of Nova Scotia by the British in 1755. The suffering of the Acadian exiles was recounted in the narrative poem Evangeline by American poet Henry Wadsworth Longfellow.

Berry reported back to the king that the plan to move the settlers was impossible. The king accepted his report and agreed to let settlers stay, but at the same time he agreed to let the fishing admirals deal with inhabitants as they wished.

For the next two years, fishing admirals endeavoured to tear down every house between Cape Race and Cape Bonavista. Migratory fishermen in the employ of West Country merchants destroyed the property of settlers, burnt forests and ruined harbours by filling them with dumped ballast.

The settlers banded together under the leadership of the four most prominent men in the colony — the aforementioned Thomas

9

The Gut was protected by the guns of the Quidi Vidi battery.

Oxford of St. John's, John Downing of Quidi Vidi, George Kirke of Ferryland, and John Pynn of Harbour Grace — and put forth the contention that a governor and increased numbers of permanent residents were necessary in order to keep the French in Placentia from taking over the whole of the island.

The arguments of the settlers, combined with reports of naval commanders that migratory fishermen were responsible for acts of destruction they blamed on settlers, led to a reprieve. Settlement was permitted, but the official hope was that it would be kept small, a token force of occupation to counter French competition in the lucrative Newfoundland fishery.

# John Downing of Quidi Vidi

*I*n the records of 1680, John Downing is included among the inhabitants of "St. John's Harbour and Quitevide." Downing was a well-to-do man who had a wife, three daughters and two women servants. He employed 15 fishermen in the winter, 12 in the summer, and owned two stages and five boats. He had two houses, one at the foot of Cochrane Street and another in Quidi Vidi where his fishing premises were located. He also had a small farm near Virginia Lake, then known as Downing's Pond.

It was Downing whom the Newfoundland settlers elected to go to King Charles ll and entreat him to stop the destruction being done by West Country fishermen.

In his petition of 1676, Downing said he had lived in Newfoundland every summer for the past 30 years. He said his father had been sent to Newfoundland to look after the colony and "reduce the Indians to civility and religion" and had died in Newfoundland after a number of years service. He continued:

*And since his death your petitioner amongst several others of your subjects hath settled there and lived for many years under the said laws and orders given them and by their industry built houses for their habitation and cleansed the wildernesses of the place, whereby to keep some cattle for their sustenance and the support of such of your Majesty's subjects as come to trade there and have of leave of the former Governor and Proprietors erected several stages and rooms for their winter and summer fisheries and support. They have hitherto lived your Majesty's obedient subjects maintaining by their own industry themselves, their wives, and their children in peace and comfort. But now some of Your Subjects, pretending Your Majesty's patent and orders for the same, coming over thither, have not only taken the houses, good stages, and rooms built and enjoyed by Your Petitioner and his father for many years last past, but spoiled the boats, keeping and breaking open the houses of the said Inhabitants at their will and pleasure contrary to the ancient laws and orders of the said place, and also to those of common humanity and the freedom which all other nations which have settled in these parts enjoy. For that the Said Inhabitants can neither enjoy the effects of their own industry nor have any security from the invasion or spoils of their neighbours. May it therefore please Your Majesty that out of Your Royal Favour, you will be pleased to command that for the future no such outrages be committed, but that Your Petitioner may enjoy such houses, stages &c. as have been built and enjoyed by his Father and himself according to the said ancient laws and orders of the place and find security for himself, his wife and family from such outrages from time to come.*

Downing asked for sufficient forts and guns to ensure the safety of settlers. He said the French were "promoting their interest more and more in Newfoundland" and pointed out, according to John Aylrod, a Waterford merchant, Placentia then had more than 250 families as well as a garrison of 400 soldiers. Downing stated the French were a very real threat as were the Dutch, who had made two successful attacks on the English in Newfoundland, in 1665 on St. John's and in 1673 on Ferryland.

Downing told the king the settlers were ill-treated and asked for the appointment of a governor as well as a minister, who would bring religion to the Newfoundland settlers and their families.

His entreaty was eloquent and well stated, but much to the dismay of settlers, the king sided with the West Country merchants who were against settlement. The end result was that the settlers were granted neither a governor, a minister, nor additional fortifications.

Rule by fishing admirals continued, with the admirals permitted to take whatever fishing premises they wanted, to levy fines and to order punishments which included whipping. In addition to the fishing admirals, there were other functionaries with even more high-sounding titles, such as the Governor of Petty Harbour and the King of Quiddy Vitty. Prowse is most unflattering in his description of these individuals. He depicts a fishing admiral in his court as dressed in a blue fishing jacket and trousers filthy with pitch, tar and fish slime and wearing on his head an old sealskin cap, robbed from a Beothuck, or bartered for a glass of rum and a stick of tobacco.

The court is a fishing stage, and the judicial seat an overturned butter tub. He says at the beginning of a trial, anyone who showed up with a large bowl of calabogus — a potent mix of rum, molasses and spruce beer — was looked upon most favourably, and the dignity of the bench was sometimes diminished by the judge falling on the floor overcome by the too-potent effects of new rum and spruce beer. At the close of a trial, judgement went in favour of the one who had the largest bowl of calabogus or paid the highest bribe.

Newfoundland continued to muddle along with the British government having no real interest in encouraging settlement. In 1793, more than 100 years after Downing pleaded the cause of beleaguered settlers, the British Undersecretary of State stood in the House of Commons and said successive English governments had considered Newfoundland simply "as a great ship moored near the Banks during the fishing season for the convenience of English fishermen."

# French Attacks

*I*n the spring of 1696 England and France were at war, and Pierre Le Moyne D'Iberville, a Canadian naval officer, received orders from De Frontenac, the governor of French Placentia, to destroy English settlements in Newfoundland. Strengthened by the arrival of Canadian Indians under orders from French officers, D'Iberville and his men marched overland from Placentia to St. John's where they burnt every house.

They did the same in Portugal Cove and Torbay, each home to three families, and in what they called "Kerividi," where nine families lived. The French proceeded to Conception Bay where they destroyed almost every community.

According to the report of Abbe Baudoin, who accompanied D'Iberville, Bay de Verde then had 14 houses; Old Perlican 19; Hant's Harbour 4; New Perlican 9; Harbour Grace 14 and Carbonear 22. When the French swept through Conception Bay only Carbonear Island, where about 200 inhabitants from as far away as St. John's had fled to and fortified, escaped unscathed. The French reported the island was inaccessible.

In January of 1705, French troops and Canadian Indians, under Governor Subercase of Placentia, once again attacked British settlements in Newfoundland.

In this attack, described as more terrible than the earlier one, many settlers were savagely murdered and houses, flakes, stages and boats were destroyed. As well, 150 young men were kidnapped and taken to Placentia where they were forced to work in the French fishery.

Settlements which came under attack included what the French called "Kitty Vitty" and referred to as well as "Quidimity," as seen in the following account. The fort mentioned is Fort William, on the site of the present Fairmont Newfoundland hotel.

*At about a league from the fort there is a small harbour, called Quidimity, where there were 72 English fishing. M. de Montigny, with some Canadians and Indians, went to take them, and there was a Reformer of the Tremblers, a Quaker, who was their commander. They asked for their parole. It was granted on condition that if anyone deserted to go to the fort, all the rest would be put to the sword, to which they consented. Some of our Indians went there occasionally to count them. As soon as the Indians came they all put themselves in a row. It happened that one day one of them wished to desert; the others followed and arrested him, and gave notice of it to the French, and without further trial or procedure, he had his head broken on the spot where he was taken.*

The man killed, according to the account of Richard Sampson, was Richard King.

Following the 1705 attack, the British placed a boom and chain at the entrance to St. John's Harbour to ensure better security. The chain was fastened to a rock still known as Chain Rock.

In a report dated January 16, 1706, Lord Dartmouth said the English living year round in Newfoundland were dispersed in 30 harbours, coves and other fishing places. He said they lived there without civil or military government anywhere except for St. John's, where there was a fort.

While the report doesn't express any concern for the settlers, there is consideration of the fact that the acting government of Her Majesty Queen Anne is not receiving its fair share of the proceeds in trade between Newfoundland and New England.

Vessels from New England were providing Newfoundland with provisions that included bread, beef, pork, flour, peas, butter, lumber and great quantities of tobacco. European commodities carried to Newfoundland included: brandy, wine, salt, hats and silks from France, brandy and iron from Spain; wine, brandy, salt, oil and linen from Portugal.

Much of these goods brought to Newfoundland ended up being illegally sold or traded. At the end of the fishing season, New England trading vessels departed Newfoundland laden with goods as well as servants of West Country merchants who had been kidnapped or enticed away with promises of better wages.

Lord Dartmouth put forth the suggestion, not acted upon at that time, that appointment of a customs collector would ensure the British government got its fair share of the proceeds from illegal trade.

The customs collector would also be able to search New England vessels to make sure they weren't leaving with more men than they had arrived with.

In 1708, settlers in Newfoundland came under attack from the French again, this time led by St. Ovide de Brouillon of Placentia. On February 2, 1709, residents of St. John's, Petty Harbour, Bay Bulls, Torbay, Portugal Cove, Perlican and Quidi Vidi signed terms of surrender in which they agreed to pay St. Ovide a ransom amounting to £7,280 on conditions including no damage be done to their stages or boats, that their houses and clothes be preserved and that the French not waste their food supplies.

On March 27, when St. Ovide departed St. John's en route to Placentia, he took seven merchants with him, including William Keen who owned property in St. John's and Quidi Vidi. St. Ovide held the merchants captive in Placentia until June 26, to ensure his ransom was paid.

**Loading dried fish near the turn of the 20th century.**

Collection of Peg Magnone

**Early morning in Quidi Vidi harbour.**

By Peter Stacey

# William Keen

*I*n 1713, the French were ousted from Placentia under the terms of the Treaty of Utrecht.

The treaty established British sovereignty in Newfoundland, allowing the French use of the shore from Cape Bonavista to Point Riche for the sole purpose of catching and drying fish. They were not permitted to erect fortifications or houses.

However, despite the pleas of Newfoundland settlers for a resident governor, rule by fishing admirals continued until 1729 when 31-year-old Captain Henry Osborne was appointed as the first in a series of naval governors. These "floating governors" stayed for the fishing season and returned to England in the fall. Osborne was an effective administrator. During his term of office he divided the island into six districts, appointed justices of the peace, built a court house and prison in St. John's and erected stocks for the punishment of petty crimes.

William Keen was appointed as one of the first justices of the peace in 1732. A few years later, in 1741, Keen was made health officer for the port of St. John's as well as judge of the vice-admiralty court.

On September 9, 1754, Keen was at his summer house in Quidi Vidi when a robbery took place. During the course of the robbery he was wounded, injuries from which he suffered and ultimately died September 29.

As told by Mike McCarthy in The Irish in Newfoundland 1600-1900 (Creative Printers 1999), the robbery was instigated by Eleanor Power, a young Irish woman who had come out from Ireland to work as a servant in Keen's house. When her term of employment was finished, she married fisherman Robert Power and moved to Blackhead, a community near St. John's.

As a result of working in Keen's house, Eleanor knew he kept a chest of gold in his house to finance his business and especially for buying ships taken as war prizes. As part of her plan to rob her former employer's house, she enlisted the help of her husband and eight other Irishmen, three of them soldiers stationed at the fort in St. John's.

The robbery was successfully carried out and Keen was thought to have been killed, but he lived long enough to identify Eleanor as one of the thieves and so all nine were captured. One of the nine, Nicholas Tobin, turned King's evidence and told how there had been two unsuccessful attempts to rob Keen prior to September 9. Both attempts failed because each time there were too many people around the house.

On the morning of September 9, it was agreed there would be another attempt to complete the robbery. The would-be robbers, including Eleanor dressed in men's clothing, began to arrive at

Keen's house in Quidi Vidi at 10 p.m. By midnight they were all in place.

The group who entered Keen's house came out bringing a case Eleanor claimed contained gold. Much to the robbers' dismay, however, when the case was opened it was found to contain French wines, not gold.

According to Tobin, one of the robbers, Edmund McGuire, said he would be revenged upon Keen for something that had happened between them some months earlier, when Keen had ordered McGuire whipped for being drunk and disorderly.

McGuire and three others then re-entered the house and went to Keen's bedroom where they found him asleep. Matthew Halleran reached under the bed and pulled out a box causing Keen to wake up. McGuire pulled the quilt over Keen's head. Keen sat up in bed and managed to put out the candle McGuire held in his hand. Keen caught Halleran by the leg and cried out "Murder." Halleran struck Keen twice with the scythe he was carrying. McGuire followed with a blow from the butt end of his musket.

At the trial, two physicians said Keen died as a result of the wounds he sustained September 9. McGuire testified he had nothing to say in his own defence and declared that only he and Halleran had been in the room when Keen was wounded. The jury took half an hour to come back with a verdict of guilty for all charged on two counts of felony and murder. The sentence passed read as follows:

> *That you Edmund McGuire, Matthew Halleran, Robert Power, Eleanor Power, Lawrence Lambly, Paul McDonald, John Moody, John Munshall and Denis Hawkins be sent back to the place from whence you came and then be hanged by the neck until you are dead, dead, dead, and the Lord have mercy upon your soul. And that Edmund McGuire and Matthew Halleran after being dead and taken down are to be hanged in chains in some public place where and when the Governor shall be pleased to appoint.*

On October 10, 1754, McGuire and Halleran were executed by hanging and their bodies taken down and hung in chains on Gibbert Hill. At noon the following day, Eleanor and Robert Power were hanged together on the end of Keen's wharf. Their bodies were buried near the place of execution. Eleanor Power was the first woman to be executed in Newfoundland.

The remaining robbers were confined to the "brig" at the fort. According to McCarthy, Lambly was later executed, but the other five prisoners received a Royal Pardon and were ordered transported out of Newfoundland in 1759.

Prowse refers to Keen's murder as a "horrible crime" and says the details, given at length in the records, are "most revolting." In the

**A sample of William Keen's Report, 1709.**
**Courtesy of the Centre for Newfoundland Studies Archives (MF - 059),**
**Memorial University of Newfoundland, St. John's, Newfoundland.**

wake of Keen's murder, penal laws making it a criminal offense for Catholics to attend mass or any religious service were strictly enforced. These harsh rules remained in effect until 1784, when Governor Campbell granted Catholics religious freedom.

Five years after Keen's murder, there was an incident which resulted in a resident of Quidi Vidi being hanged for his part in the illegal act of stealing a cow. According to author Jack Fitzgerald in Beyond Belief: Stories of Old St. John's (Creative Publishers 2001), William Gilmore had operated a successful business in his home in Quidi Vidi selling liquor to soldiers from Fort William in St. John's. His downfall came in April of 1759 after he encouraged two friends to steal and kill one of the cows grazing in a meadow now occupied by Government House.

Gilmore planned the crime and arranged to hide the meat in his well. His two accomplices killed the cow but left the knife that Gilmore had given them at the scene of the deed. When the knife was found, Gilmore's wife identified it as belonging to her husband. Within days there was a trial and Gilmore was executed at Gallows Hill on the corner of Queen's Road and Barter's Hill. The records are not clear on what happened to the other two. Fitzgerald notes in the 18th century there were more than 122 crimes for which a person could be executed, and one of these was the stealing of a cow.

# Battle of 1762

*I*n 1756, Newfoundland had a permanent population of about 6,000 and Britain and France were once again at war. To the French, Newfoundland, and in particular St. John's, where there was a single company of 63 soldiers and existing forts were in a state of decay, seemed an ideal target for attack.

In the spring of 1762, the French government sent out four ships of war, 32 officers and approximately 700 troops under the command of Count D' Haussonville. The French landed in Bay Bulls on June 24, 1762, and marched overland to St. John's where the small British garrison was forced to surrender without giving resistance or obtaining terms.

French troops immediately set to work repairing the fortifications, erecting fresh defences on Signal Hill, and building two gun batteries at Quidi Vidi to defend Signal Hill from a rear attack. The French also sailed into Conception Bay, captured Harbour Grace and Carbonear, and went on to take Trinity.

Ten weeks after the French invasion, a British fleet under Rear Admiral Lord Colville, commander of the British North American Squadron, arrived off the coast of Newfoundland with what Prowse says were less than 700 troops under Lieutenant-Colonel William Amherst.

The English attempted to land at Quidi Vidi, but the French had blocked the harbour entrance by sinking a number of light boats (shallops). On September 13, the British landed at Torbay, about eight miles north of St. John's. The French tried to stop the landing, but the British light infantry, under a Captain McDonell, soon drove them back. The British marched along a narrow path leading to St. John's for about four miles, then passed through a thick wood, over some very rough ground, and continued on towards Quidi Vidi where Amherst regrouped his troops at a farm called the Grove, on the site of present-day Pleasantville.

Amherst himself described what happened next in a dispatch dated September 20, 1762.

*We marched to the left of Kitty Vitty. It was necessary to take possession of this pass to open a communication for the landing of artillery and stores, it being impracticable to get them up the way we came. As soon as our right was close to Kitty Vitty river, the enemy fired upon us from a hill on the opposite side. I sent a party up a rock, which commanded the passage over, and under cover of their fire, the light infantry companies of the Royal and Montgomery's, supported by the grenadiers of the Royal, passed, drove the enemy up the hill, and pursued them on that side towards St. John's, when I perceived a body of the enemy coming to their support, and immediately ordered up Major Sutherland, with the remainder of the first battalion, upon* which they thought proper to retreat, and we had just time before dark to take post. Captain Mackenzie, who commanded Montgomery's light infantry, was badly wounded. We took ten prisoners. The troops lay this night on their arms.

The next morning, the 14th, we opened the channel, where the enemy had sunk the shallops; they had a breast work which commanded the entrance, and a battery not quite finished. Lieutenant-Colonel Tullikin, who had met with an accident by a fall, and was left on board, joined me this day, and Captain Ferguson, commanding the artillery, brought round some light artillery and stores from Torbay, in the shallops. The enemy had possession of two very high and steep hills, one in the front of our advanced posts, and the other nearer to St. John's, which two hills appeared to command the whole ground from Kitty Vitty to St. John's. It was necessary that we should proceed on this side, to secure at the same time effectually the landing at the Kitty Vitty; from the first hill the enemy fired upon our posts. On the 15th, just before daybreak, I ordered Captain McDonell's corps of light infantry, and the provincial light infantry, supported by our advanced posts, to march to surprise the enemy on this hill. Captain McDonell passed their sentries and advanced guards, and was first discovered by their main body on the hill as he came climbing up the rocks near the summit, which he gained, receiving the enemy's fire. He threw in his fire, and the enemy gave way. Captain McDonell was wounded, Lieutenant Schuyler of his company killed, and three or four men, and 18 wounded. The enemy had three companies of grenadiers, and two picquets at this post, commanded by Lieutenant-Colonel Belcombe, second in command, who was wounded; a captain of grenadiers wounded and taken prisoner, his lieutenant killed, several men killed and wounded, and 13 taken prisoner. The enemy had one mortar here, with which they threw some shells at us in the night; a six-pounder not mounted, and two wall pieces. This hill, with one adjoining, commands the harbour.

The 16th we advanced to the hill nearer St. John's, which the enemy had quitted. Twenty-nine shallops came in today with artillery and stores, provision and camp equipage, from Torbay, which we unloaded . I moved the remainder of the troops forward, leaving a post to guard the pass of Kitty Vitty on the other side. Last night the enemy's fleet got out of the harbour. This night we lay on our arms.

The 17th a mortar battery was completed and a battery begun for four 24-pounders and two 12-pounders; about 400 yards from the fort made the road from the landing for the artillery, and at night opened the mortar battery with one 8-inch mortar, seven cohorns and six royals. The enemy fired pretty briskly from the fort and threw in some shells.

20

On September 16, Amherst had a letter delivered to Count D'Haussonville at Fort William giving him half an hour to think about surrendering the fort. The French commander wrote back that he had no intention of surrendering. Two days later, however, on May 18, he changed his mind and consented to surrender the fort under conditions that included approximately 700 French soldiers at the fort be declared prisoners of war and provided with ships to carry them home to France. Amherst agreed with the conditions. On the 20th the whole French garrison surrendered. Prowse notes, on page 309, that Captain McDonell, hero of the assault on Signal Hill, was nursed back to health by Mrs. Horwood of Quidi Vidi, "great-grandmother of Mr. John Horwood, best known amongst us as "Protestant John, of Quidi Vidi." Although he was severely wounded, McDonell finally recovered and returned to England.

Grove Farm, where Amherst paused to regroup, was established by British Lieutenant Griffith Williams, who was stationed at Carbonear Island in 1745 and later promoted to St. John's where he commanded the Royal Artillery and lived for 12 to 14 years.

In 1757, he acquired a grant of 200 acres of land from Governor Edwards and established a farm he named Golden Grove after a family estate in Wales. When the French took St. John's, Golden Grove was pillaged and the buildings destroyed, but Williams later restored the property. After he left Newfoundland and was away on foreign service, he wrote the governor that he anticipated coming back and making his farm flourish. He said Colonel Skinner, commanding officer at Fort William, had married a member of his family and founded a place west of Grove Farm called Cottage Farm which was, at that time, occupied by a Mr. Ross. Williams told the governor Grove Farm and Cottage Farm took up nearly the whole of the north side of Quidi Vidi Lake.

After leaving Newfoundland, Williams served with the British in the American War of Independence and attained the rank of general. A writer as well as a soldier, in 1765 he published an account in which he noted from the years 1745 to 1752 the combined settlements of "Kidvide," Torbay, St. John's, and Petty Harbour accounted for one quarter of Newfoundland's entire fishery. Remarking on the state of fortifications in Newfoundland, he said:

*St. John's from 1745 to 1750 was very well garrisoned by four companies of Foot, a captain of artillery with about 50 men. It was also well supplied with all manner of stores and about 40 pieces of cannon. Feriland, Carboniere and Trinity Harbours had each an officer of artillery with about 18 to 20 men and an officer of Foot and 30 men. There were 200 small arms at each place for the use of the Inhabitants. If those defences had been kept up the French would not have succeeded in capturing those places in 1762.*

21

# Mallard Cottage

*T*oday, at 2 Barrows Road in Quidi Vidi, there's a charming cottage which, if only it could talk, would be able to hold us spellbound with tales of long ago days. If Mallard Cottage was indeed built in the 1750s, as is argued by some history buffs, it may well have been used in some official capacity during those bloody battles between the French and the British. The house in which Captain McDonell was nursed back to health by Mrs. Horwood is said to have been near the church, not far away.

Mallard Cottage now belongs to Peg Magnone, an English-born great-grandmother who restored it as a combination home and business. Mallard Cottage Antiques and Collectibles is a place where you can find everything from one-of-a-kind puffin postcards to old books, china, pictures and prints.

Peg is a woman with a definite spirit of adventure who has lived and worked in Canada's far north and in Mexico. An ex-school-teacher, she was 64 and twice divorced when she moved from British Columbia and came to Newfoundland in 1986.

Her initial visit to Newfoundland was to see her daughter, Stephanie, and her family who had recently settled here. While in the St. John's area, Peg visited Quidi Vidi where she fell in love with Mallard Cottage, saw it was up for sale, and impulsively decided to buy it.

Returning to British Columbia, which had been her home for more than 20 years, she sold her house and loaded all her worldly possessions into and on top of two vans. Towing the vans, she spent 13 days driving from the west coast to the east, sleeping at night on the floor of one vehicle. She recalls the cross-country trek as a hair-raising experience mainly because she was unable to back up. She could move her trailer–like contraption forward but not in reverse.

Peg bought Mallard Cottage from a nephew of Agnes Mallard, the last in a long line of Mallards to live in the house. The nephew put the cottage up for sale following his aunt's death.

When Peg purchased Mallard Cottage there was no water, no power and no bathroom. Undaunted, she began restoration work. In the midst of her work she wrote a poem about the layers of wallpaper that had helped to insulate the cottage from winter cold, the 100-year-old cache of bottles she found beneath the floor, the soldier's button wedged behind a chimney brick, and the fire tongs she discovered boarded up beneath the stairs. She described as well the low ceiling beams and small window panes through which so many generations had peered.

Today, a visit to Mallard Cottage Antiques and Collectibles is like stepping back in time. A bell rings as you go through the narrow front door and step down into a small front porch with low-ceilinged room on either side. The cottage has all original windows and doors. There's a stone fireplace in the middle of the building

**Painting of Mallard Cottage, Quidi Vidi, by Arthur Andrews**
On November 27, 1939, 20-year-old Arthur Andrews of Winterton was among the first draft of naval recruits who departed St. John's on the RMS Newfoundland enroute to help England win the Second World War. After the war, he settled in St. John's where he married and spent 30 years working at The Evening Telegram as a cartoonist.
Now a resident of Caribou Memorial Veteran's Pavilion on Forest Road, Art is a man of many talents. An accomplished painter and poet, his most ambitious poetic effort is The Dream of Orno, a 338-page prose poem that took him 12 years to complete.
One of Art's favourite activities used to be taking long, rambling walks through the hills around Quidi Vidi village and stopping to sketch or paint whatever caught his eye.

and there are two hearths, one on each floor. The original structure of the house was rectangular and there were four rooms, two on the first floor and two on the second. The second floor rooms are lit by windows set at floor level beneath the eaves.

An addition at the back, serving as a kitchen, now extends to one side of the first floor and, at the back, Peg has added on a room to hold her ever growing collectibles. The lower floor rooms are filled with a fascinating assortment that includes, pictures, prints, books, china, glassware, jewellery, buttons, brass, pewter, coins, stamps and old post cards.

Peg says Mallard Cottage was built by two Mallard brothers who came out from Ireland to pursue a new life as dairy farmers. If the brothers could once again walk along the roads of Quidi Vidi and stand before the house they built they'd likely be pleased to see how very little it has changed through the years. And while it is interesting to speculate the cottage was constructed in about 1750, the truth is it was more likely built somewhere between 1820 and 1840. Mallard Cottage has been designated as a historic site by the Historic Sites and Monuments Board of Canada and also by the Heritage Foundation of Newfoundland and Labrador.

# Poetry in Praise of Quidi Vidi

*T*houghts on Mallard Cottage, Quidi Vidi, During Restoration,
the poem Peg Magnone wrote in 1989.

*The years dissolve miraculously*
*Two centuries come alive for me*
*Beneath my probing tools*
*Old ghosts arise and share my chores*
*I ask them "is this mine or yours?"*
*They smile their enigmatic smiles*
*That beckon me across the miles*
*Of hopes and dreams and endless toil*
*That caused this house to be*
*The joys they shared with family*
*And, too, the hours of misery*

*As I climb the steep, worn stairway*
*Up to my cosy bed*
*I ponder on the families*
*Who trod where now I tread*
*Who carved those Roman numerals*
*On sloping boards of fir?*
*So slowly now revealed to me*
*'Neath paper layer on layer*
*Each pattern chosen lovingly*
*By "Mallard" women kind*
*Without a thought of heritage*
*That they would leave behind*
*Layers that helped to insulate*
*Against Atlantic cold*
*And winds from Quidi Vidi Gut*
*Through winters all untold*

*Who forgot the fire tongs*
*Boarded beneath the stair*
*Of the staircase to the bedrooms*
*For me to find them there?*
*The fine old centre chimney brick*
*Begins to crumble dust*
*Revealing a soldier's button*
*Without a trace of rust*

**Mallard Cottage**

By Peter Stacey

*How did it come to be wedged away*
*For me to wonder on today?*

*No square corners— no level floors*
*Latches instead of knobs on doors*
*A cache of bottles 'neath the floor*
*Been there a hundred years or more*
*Stand now in sparkling array*
*Adding such pleasure today*
*Repairs become more like excavation*
*And each new find a revelation*

*Strong ceiling beams – so very low*
*Small window-panes in moonlight's glow*
*How many women have waited there*
*Watching, listening and wondering where*
*Menfolk and children are today?*
*Some things are constant anyway*
*Like birth and death this house has known*
*And seeds of kindness gently sown*

*Old house you live and breathe like me*
*And hold your place in history*
*A heritage of Newfoundland*
*Helping us to understand*
*Those pioneers from Ireland*
*So far across the sea*
*The story of a hardy folk*
*And how "we" came to be*

Others who have penned a few lines about the picturesque village include Reverend Michael Francis Howley, the first native-born Newfoundlander to become a Roman Catholic bishop.

The fourth of 13 children of Irish immigrants, Howley was born in St. John's in 1843 and died in 1914. His poem about Quidi Vidi was short and to the point:

> *Oh, just behind the city*
> *In a vale so bright and pretty*
> *Lies the lovely Kitty Vitty.*
> *Basking in the summer day.*

Newfoundland historian George Story came across a much longer poem which took up the whole of a 14- page book he spotted and bought while browsing through a bookstore in Nova Scotia.

The Rocks of Quidi Vidi contained 455 lines of verse by an author who neglected to include his or her name. Writing in the spring 1986 issue of Newfoundland Studies, Story said he figured the author was from Quidi Vidi and born somewhere between 1815 and 1825. He speculated the poem was written between 1860 and 1870 based on particular references to Martin Luther and John Knox, religious reformers of the 1500s.

The following is an excerpt from Part 1 of The Rocks of Quidi Vidi:

> *Can spot of earth so pleasant be,*
> *As Quidi Vidi rocks to me*
> *On whose wild crags I oft have leaned*
> *And in whose little church have gleaned*
> *Fruits to refresh me on the way*
> *And hopes the startling tear to stay.*

Part 3, the final part of the poem reads:

> *Hail! Quidi Vidi, dear to me*
> *Are thy bold crags, they pathways free;*
> *'Twere bliss to climb those steeps again,*
> *And gaze from thence upon the main;*
> *'Twere bliss among thy rocks to wonder,*
> *And by thy beauteous lakes to ponder*
> *Where, cradled in their beds of green,*
> *Thy sparkling waters, aye, are seen;*
> *Heavens own pure rays upon them becoming*
> *On night's bright eyes above them gleaming*

# Construction Underway

*I*n 1764, when Sir Hugh Palliser was Newfoundland's acting naval governor, a move to halt illegal smuggling between Newfoundland and New England resulted in a collector of customs being appointed in St. John's. As well, an act was passed which armed Custom House authorities with powers of seizure and arrest and gave a bounty directly to the governor and the informer, with His Excellency getting one third of the plunder.

In 1765, at the end of Palliser's four years as naval governor, he reported the resident population of Newfoundland: men, 9,976; women, 1,645; children, 3,863. Total: 15,484. When more than 9,000 migratory fishermen arrived for the fishing season the population increased to over 25,000.

The end of the Seven Years War (1756-1763) between England and France resulted in the expulsion of France from North America.

But, as a result of the 1763 Treaty of Paris, France retained the French Shore from Cape Bonavista to Point Riche in Newfoundland, and was legally ceded the islands of St-Pierre-et-Miquelon. This, coupled with the seriousness of the French attack on Newfoundland in 1762, guaranteed the continuing presence of British army garrisons.

Britain wasn't particularly worried about the safety of Newfoundland settlers. In 1766, Secretary of State, the Duke of Richmond, noted "the protection of the inhabitants settled on the island is neither practicable nor desirable." What he wanted was a safe port with a small garrison where British fishermen could retreat in the event of an attack by the French.

On the advice of Captain Hugh Debbieg of the Royal Engineers, who was sent to find the most likely harbour where British vessels fishing on the Newfoundland coast could safely retreat in the case of a sudden attack, it was decided to construct a new fortification on ground to the west of Fort William.

The new fort would command the landward approaches from the west and be out of range of guns the enemy might place on Signal Hill. It would also command the harbour and be well suited to defend the town from either land or sea attack. Debbieg also suggested a tower be built at the entrance to the Narrows to provide early protection to fishing vessels fleeing from an enemy attack.

As a result of his recommendations, Amherst Tower was built at the south side of the Narrows entrance and Fort Townshend was situated on the high ground west of Fort William.

On page 336, Prowse remarks on construction underway in St. John's in 1773 and notes the way in which title to land was acquired:

Re-enactment at Quidi Vidi Battery

*In 1773 Fort Townshend was commenced and the road to it from the Queen's Wharf, also the King's Road, the Military Road between Fort William and Fort Townshend, and the Signal Hill Road. (It is) curiously illustrative of the corruption and favouritism which prevailed in the days of our naval governors: all around Fort William officers and soldiers had been allowed to take in land as far as the margin of Quidi Vidi Lake; on removal, soldiers and officers sold these to civilians in the town; valuable properties, both on the south and north side of Water Street, were purchased sometimes for a winter's provisions; a good building lot on the north side of Water Street, east of McBride's Hill, was given to one large firm for their cook's passage to England. Stripling, a stout Protestant and a publican, through the interests of the officers and soldiers, obtained a piece of land at Quidi Vidi, and afterwards, when he became a justice and sheriff, though utterly ignorant and illiterate, a grant of land on the east side of King's Bridge Road, and all Stripling's plantation, were given to him.*

Some members of the military fenced and cleared their tracts of land and planted gardens in which they grew potatoes and other root vegetables. A map of St. John's and Quidi Vidi in 1772 shows such enclosures scattered around Fort William and also indicates other enclosed land, perhaps belonging to the military, at the head of Quidi Vidi harbour and on the north side of the lake, where Golden Grove farm was located.

# The United States, a New Nation

On July 4, 1776, 13 British colonies on the eastern seaboard of North America declared their independence from their mother country, heralding the creation of a new nation, the United States of America.

In July of 1778, France recognized the independence of the United States, and declared war on England. All through 1780, St. John's was kept in a state of vigilance. Due to the fear of an enemy attack from either the French or the Americans, batteries were established at Quidi Vidi, Cuckhold's Cove, Amherst Tower, Frederick's Battery, Chain Rock Battery, Fort William, Fort Townshend, Petty Harbour, and in the Torbay and Bay Bulls Roads. As well, a ship was moored at River Head to defend the path leading into St. John's from Bay Bulls.

In 1782, Britain acknowledged the independence of the United States, and not long afterwards went from war with the States and her allies, France, Spain and Holland, into a long war with France. When the French Revolution began in 1789, public sentiment in Great Britain at first favoured it, but as the revolutionary government became terroristic, the British public and political leaders turned against it and war was declared once more against France in 1793.

The French armies were overwhelmingly successful, particularly when command was given to Napoleon Bonaparte, later Napoleon I. By 1796 with her allies Spain, Austria, Prussia and Sardinia defeated, England was left alone to fight Bonaparte.

There was great consternation in St. John's when a French fleet appeared off Cape Spear in September 1796. The naval governor, Sir James Wallace, immediately proclaimed martial law and mustered the newly formed Royal Newfoundland Regiment and as many other men as he could. By daylight on September 2, tents were pitched on the summit of Signal Hill, from the Duke of York's battery to Cuckhold Head and on the Southside Hills over Fort Amherst. Later in the day seaman worked at stretching the great chain across the entrance to the Narrows and fastening it to Chain Rock.

This warlike show and the display of more than 3,000 men on Signal Hill so intimidated the French that they finally sailed away, stopping en route to destroy Bay Bulls. In France, reports of this incident proclaimed that French Admiral Richery had landed 1,500 men at Bay Bulls, 2,000 at Portugal Cove and had captured a large number of ships and fishing vessels, as well as 1,000 sailors, who had been sent to St. Domingo.

England prosecuted the war against Napoleon vigorously. The British fleet under Admiral Horatio Nelson defeated the French fleet at Trafalgar; the Duke of Wellington drove the French armies out of Portugal and Spain in the Peninsular War and, after the disastrous retreat of Napoleon from Moscow, he was defeated at Leipzig in 1813 and at Waterloo in 1815.

Britain's war with France coincided with a second struggle with the United States, the War of 1812. During the whole of this conflict, Newfoundland was in a state of great prosperity. Prowse notes, on page 387, that wages were high, the price received for fish and oil was also "abnormally high" and the harbour in St. John's was full of captured American "prizes," vessels laden with valuable freight, everything from Lyons silk to whole cargoes of champagne.

The clerks at Hunt, Stabb, Preston & Co., the company acting as agents for the vessels, spent their Sunday afternoon firing at champagne bottles. The man who knocked the head off the bottle won a case, the one who missed had to pay for them.

NH -- New Hampshire
M -- Massachusetts
C -- Connecticut
R -- Rhode Island
NJ -- New Jersey
ML -- Maryland
D -- Delaware
━ ━ ━ Boundaries of U.S.A. as established by the Treaty of Versailles
- - - - Boundaries between colonies before independence

0   100 200 300 400 500 miles

0    200   400   600   800 km

# Quidi Vidi in 1794

*I*n 1780-81, a 12-foot road was cut from the back of Fort William, the Old Garrison, to the "Quiddy Viddy Hills" for the benefit of cattle. In 1794, the census records Quidi Vidi as having a population of 38 men, 19 women, 49 children — 33 boys and 16 girls — as well as 24 hired fishermen, six women servants and 29 dieters (men given board and lodging in return for work preparing for the fishery).

The population of 165 was made up of 106 Catholics and 59 Protestants. The majority of the householders were tenants on land owned by merchants operating in nearby St. John's, and most were almost exclusively engaged in the fishery.

Twenty-six of the 38 men were recorded as fishermen, including Thomas, Phil and George Brace and Michael Newall, all of whom were born in Newfoundland. Among the other fishermen was John Reardon, who operated out of a fishing room owned by Newfoundland's Chief Justice, D'Ewes Coke.

Others living in the village included five shoremen: William Davis, Pat Nowlan, William Pendergrass, James Dohoney, and James Noonan; one boat keeper, James Costello, who was Newfoundland-born; James Henneberry, a carpenter, also born in Newfoundland; a cooper named Ed Hearne; a butcher by the name of Robert Brine, and farmers Michael Curren and John Ryan.

Quidi Vidi of 1794 was described in the journal of Aaron Thomas, an able seaman on "The Boston," which arrived in St. John's Harbour on August 25, 1794. Thomas wrote:

> *There is a road to Titti Whitti through the woods. On the left hand side is the large lake of Titti Whitti, and from it runs a stream of water of some magnitude. Before it falls into the sea it forms a cascade, it then meanders through and under some fish flakes and falls into the ocean in a little cove called Titti Whitti Cove. There are seven or eight houses and fish flakes down in a hole which forms a kind of amphitheatre; the rocks round it rise to a great height.*
>
> *The day being warm, on my arrival there my nose was refreshed with a fragrant smell, which is very common to this country, and the best of the business was that I met with the flavour in its highest perfection. Most of the fish rooms in Newfoundland are built so that the cutting is over the water. The fish, which are daily brought ashore, are operated upon in the cutting room, where their heads and filth are thrown into the water. This offal the tyde carries away. At Titti Whitti these conveniences cannot be adapted, for the fish rooms, flakes etc. are upon broken rocks and barren spots. The cod's heads and offal are thrown on dry land, where they get putrid and breed maggots and in this putridness send forth a most offensive smell which far exceeds the effluvia arising from a collection of the bones of horses in the environs of an Ivory Black Manufactory.*

31

# Good Times Precede the Bad

*A*s a result of the Napoleonic Wars involving France and Great Britain and the 1812 war between Great Britain and the United States, Newfoundland's two greatest fishing competitors, France and New England, had to vacate the coast leaving the fishing grounds to Newfoundland fishermen and the few English ships that might venture across the Atlantic. For three years, Newfoundland enjoyed a monopoly of the fishery and the markets. Fish were abundant, the weather was favourable and prosperity was in the air.

Reports of the economic good times encouraged many people in Europe, particularly the impoverished Irish, to come to Newfoundland and seek their fortunes. Nearly 7,000 people, most from southeast Ireland, arrived in Newfoundland in 1814 and a further 4,000 came the following year.

In 1815, the end of the wars with France and the United States brought unprecedented hardship and disaster to Newfoundland. With the arrival of peace, French and

**The window of Mallard cottage: modern reflections on history.**

By Peter Stacey

American fishermen returned to their normal fishing grounds. The result was that the price of fish fell by half, then went even lower.

Merchants in Newfoundland, who had contracted with suppliers and workers when prices were at their highest, found themselves unable to meet their obligations. Firm after firm went bankrupt and those that remained had little credit. The thousands of new arrivals who had come during the boom years found themselves without work or resources. For Newfoundland, the post-war years were ones of famine, bitter cold and terrible fires.

During the winter of 1817, St. John's was devastated by a fire which left 1,000 people homeless. The following November, fires in the town resulted in the destruction of hundreds of buildings and left a further 2,000 people homeless. The fires destroyed houses as well as many businesses, including most of the warehouses containing the colony's food supplies.

The bitterly cold winter of 1817-1818 became known as the Winter of the Rals, from an Irish word for rowdies, and referring to the roaming gangs of half-starved, lawless men, deserters, discharged servants, men with no employment and no family obligations, who everywhere threatened life and property as they tried to steal what little food was available.

During the Winter of the Rals, many people died of starvation or froze to death for want of a proper place to live. Among those who died during the harsh winter of 1818 was Admiral Francis Pickmore, who had been appointed as Newfoundland's first resident governor the year before. Pickmore's death in a cold, drafty house at Fort Townshend in St. John's resulted in him acquiring the dubious distinction as the first resident governor to die in office in Newfoundland.

Until the end of the 18th century, settlers in Newfoundland were legally unable to enclose land or to build houses without permission. This matter was finally brought to a head by large-scale immigration from Ireland, and after 1813 the governors were allowed to grant land for cultivation.

Instructions from England to Sir Richard Keats, the naval governor, were that all "residents and industrious inhabitants desirous of obtaining small grants of land for the purpose of cultivation in the neighbourhood of St. John's, subject to very moderate quit-rent, are desired to give in their applications to the office of the Secretary to the Governor, before the last day of July."

Keats later reported back that more than 1,000 acres were in cultivation and many more had been enclosed. Produce being grown included hay, potatoes and other vegetables.

The first post office in Newfoundland was established in 1805 with Simon Solomon as Postmaster-General. The Benevolent Irish Society was formed in St. John's in 1806. That same year, Newfoundland's first newspaper, the Royal Gazette and Newfoundland Advertiser, was published by John Ryan, an American loyalist. In about 1815, the first schools were opened at St. John's. By the end of 1815, when the British government finally recognized Newfoundland as open for settlement, the island had its own administrative establishment, a court house, and churches. Between 1800 and 1832, the population of Newfoundland grew rapidly. There were less than 20,000 residents on the island in 1800. By 1832, the population was 60,000.

# A Fatal Duel

*I*n 1829, a fatal duel was fought in St. John's which had a connection to Quidi Vidi. In March 1829, officers at Fort Townshend were gambling at cards when a young ensign named Philpot made a foolish move which resulted in his becoming quarrelsome.

His losses at the table coupled with too much to drink led to his being very rude to a Captain Rudkin. The upshot was that Rudkin finally challenged Philpot to a duel.

According to historian Paul O'Neill, the underlying reason for Philpot's behaviour was that both he and Rudkin were rivals for the charms of a young Irish woman who lived in a cottage near Quidi Vidi,

On the morning of March 20, Philpot and Rudkin met in a clearing near Brine's Tavern at Robinson's Hill. Within a very short time revolvers were drawn, a shot rang out, and Philpot lay upon the ground, shot dead by Rudkin.

Captain Rudkin was subsequently arrested because duelling was forbidden by law. He was brought before a judge and jury, but despite the judge's urging to bring in a verdict of guilty the jury declared Rudkin "not guilty."

Some say that Rudkin, out of pity, took Philpot's elderly mother under his wing and cared for her for the rest of her life. What happened with the young lady from Quidi Vidi remains hidden in the mists of time.

What was her name? Was she beautiful? Did she have a broken heart when she learned of Philpot's unfortunate demise? Perhaps she married Captain Rudkin and settled down with him and Philpot's mother to raise a family somewhere on the hills above Quidi Vidi.

Writer Jack Fitzgerald has a story of another incident involving Quidi Vidi that took place sometime in the early 1800s.

It began when a pirate ship attempted to evade capture by the British Navy by pulling into Quidi Vidi harbour. The pirates carried a treasure of silver and gold to a site adjacent to Quidi Vidi Lake and buried it with plans to return to recover it at a later date. In 1870 one of the pirates returned to claim the treasure for himself. While he was in St. John's he stayed at the home of a Mr. O'Regan who operated a shoe store in the west end of the city. Before he had a chance to search for the buried treasure the pirate became sick and died, but not before telling his friend where the treasure was buried and providing a map showing where it could be found.

The map described Bennett's Grove, a spot adjacent to Quidi Vidi Lake in the vicinity of Drilling Brook, east of the boathouse. O'Regan spent days digging and when he later left for the United States there were those who said he took a portion, if not all, of the treasure with him. Another man, Kenneth Connors, also looked for the buried treasure and it was said he died of a heart attack after being approached by a misty figure with a sword.

# Christ Church

Quidi Vidi may have had its first church as early as 1777, when a Congregationalist church is thought to have been built on or near the site of the present day building.

In 1834, in an early example of ecumenicalism, the Congregationalists, Anglicans, and Methodists dedicated a new church on the site in Quidi Vidi. The land on which the church was built was purchased from village residents George, William and Richard Brace.

The ecumenical experiment was eventually abandoned, as was the church. A number of years later, with the building in a sorry state of decay, architect James Purcell designed a new church. Christ Church, opened by the Anglicans in 1842, likely incorporated part of the original structure and served a congregation of 200.

The first service was held in the still-not-completed church on November 9, 1842. There were between 30 and 40 communicants and approximately £8 was taken up in a collection. Rev. T. Bridge officiated and his address to the congregation was published in the St. John's Times:

> *The building which is cruciform is from a design kindly furnished by Mr. Purcell to Mr. H. Brett, formerly in the establishment of Messrs. W. and H. Thomas and Company – a young man of whom, we must say without impropriety, as he is no longer a resident among us, that it is to his liberal and active exertions that the people of Quidi Vidi owe much of the privileges they now enjoy.*
>
> *Though it is not yet completed this church promises to be quite a model for a village church. The communion, reading desk and pulpit are hung with purple velvet neatly and appropriately worked by some ladies of this parish.*

In 1888, the church was closed for six months while the building underwent extensive repairs and a fence was erected around the outside. A bell and tower were added in 1890.

The first bell ringers at Christ Church were Rich, Emmann, and Freddie Pynn, fishermen like their father, Joe, who came to Newfoundland from England and settled in Quidi Vidi sometime during the 1800s.

The Pynn family once had extensive land holdings in Quidi Vidi, much of it granted to Sir Frederick Carrell during the Boer War, and later bought by the Pynns, who were related to Carrell, Lady Carrell being Elizabeth Pynn. Prowse refers to the Pynns as one of the oldest English families in Newfoundland.

In 1931, Christ Church was used for the on-location filming of The Viking, the first sound feature film made in Canada and one

Tucked among the stages and flakes in this postcard detail sits Christ Church, built in the early 1800s.

of the world's first sound synchronized films shot entirely on location. The creator of the film, a young man by the name of Varrick Frissell, was born in Boston, educated at Yale University, and later volunteered to work with the International Grenfell Association in Labrador and St. Anthony.

In 1925, Frissell explored Labrador and shot the first motion picture film of Churchill Falls.

He became a member of the Royal Geographical Society and made documentary shorts on Labrador and the Newfoundland seal fishery.

In 1930, he formed the Newfoundland Labrador Film Company and started production of White Thunder, his first dramatic talkie. The movie, starring Charles Starrett, who went on to become a major cowboy actor, was about two sealers vying for the same woman. It was filmed during the annual Newfoundland seal hunt.

Frissell, along with his cast and crew, shipped out to the ice fields on the SS Ungava, skippered by legendary Arctic explorer Captain Bob Bartlett of Brigus, who had a part in the film.

The movie was completed and shown at the Nickel Theatre in St. John's on March 5, 1931, but 28-year-old Frissell was not happy with the final result. He felt the movie needed more action shots so he and his film crew decided to return to the seal hunt to shoot more footage. He envisioned dramatic shots of huge icebergs toppling over.

On March 9, 1931, Captain Abram Kean, junior, was in command when the SS Viking, owned by Bowring Bros, left St. John's en route to the seal hunt. On board was a crew of 147, plus two stowaways, a well as Frissell and his film crew. The Neptune was the first vessel to leave port, closely followed by the Viking, Beothic, Ungava, Neptune, Eagle and the almost-new Imogene. Also en route to the ice were the Thetis, Terra Nova and the Ranger.

On March 15, while the Viking was in heavy ice off the Horse Islands, an explosion ripped through the vessel killing 24 people, including Frissell and his crew. The cause of the explosion is thought to be explosives which had been brought on board by the film crew, either flares used for night photography or dynamite to create dramatic scenes.

The movie White Thunder was renamed The Viking to capitalize on public interest in the disaster. It premiered in New York on June 16, 1931, but failed at the box office. Christ Church figures prominently in the final scene of the movie when a group of half-frozen sealers thought lost at the ice fields stumble into the church as the congregation is halfway though a service.

Christ Church was for many years the focal part of village life, carefully tended by the Anglicans of Quidi Vidi. Catholics generally worshipped at the Basilica in St. John's up until the 20th century, when St. Joseph's Church was built at the foot of Signal Hill.

By 1966, the Anglican population of Quidi Vidi had declined and modern transportation made it easy for those remaining to attend church in St. John's. With Christ Church in a state of disrepair it was decided to demolish it for safety reasons. What happened then, as Shannie Duff explained in the March/April 1975 issue of Canadian Antique Collector magazine, was that a handful of people led by Edythe Goodridge, then president of the Newfoundland Art Association, met in June 1966, and decided to form an organization to try to save Christ Church and focus public concern into effective action.

The organization that grew from that meeting became The Newfoundland Historic Trust and it was through their efforts that the small church in Quidi Vidi was renovated and opened as a community centre in 1972. The church today, looking much the same as when it was first built, is a private dwelling and not open to the public.

# The Inn of Olde

*A*round the same time as Christ Church was under construction in 1842, two houses were being built not far away, on the other side of the road. One house was for the Mallard family, the other for the Henneburys. The houses today have been incorporated into an establishment known as the Inn of Olde. Situated on a curve of the main road that runs through the village, the inn is owned by Linda and Robert Hennebury.

One part of the property is the Hennebury house where Robert was born and raised, where he and Linda raised their three children and where he and Linda still live. The other part of the establishment is the Mallard house which the Henneburys bought in 1977 and turned into a pub.

Robert Hennebury is one of seven children born to Jack and Florence (Thorne). His paternal grandfather, John Hennebury, was a veteran of the First World War, a stretcher bearer who spent three years and six months in a German prisoner of war camp before returning home to Quidi Vidi.

In 1997, 20 years after the Hennebury's opened the Inn of Olde, CBC-TV host Wayne Ronstad featured it in his On the Road series in a segment called "Linda's World."

Linda is a small, dark-haired woman — a Harding from Portugal Cove — and the inn is truly her world. Although Bob also works in the inn, six days a week from noon until well after midnight, it is more than likely Linda who you will find behind the bar working away and doing her favourite thing, which is chatting with customers.

On the wall behind the bar there are well over 1,000 collector spoons that customers have sent to Linda. She says she bought the first spoon in 1980 and hasn't purchased one since. Underneath the glass that covers the top of the bar there are hundreds of business cards from all over the world, attesting to the wide variety of customers who have made it a point to visit the Inn of Olde.

Linda has other collections as well, including hundreds of buttons, mugs, 300 hats, license plates, military memorabilia, and an assortment of clowns that have a special place on shelves behind the bar. She has old bottles, fishing gear, radios, sewing machines, photographs of airplanes, typewriters, telephones, hockey memorabilia, maps drawn on toilet paper, and a seat from St. John's now-closed Memorial Stadium. Another one of Linda's collections consists of pictures of customers, including an autographed photograph of CTV's Mike Duffy.

The inn has a jukebox, there's a patio garden outside, and one of Linda's most prized possession is the plaque on the wall that she received for writing Canadian soldiers during the Persian Gulf War.

**Famous in media and in the hearts of thousands, the Quidi Vidi Inn of Olde is owned and operated by Robert and Linda Hennebury.**

The plaque is in appreciation from the Canadian Naval Task Force to whom she personally wrote almost 1,000 letters to keep up their morale. Linda considers the Inn of Olde a museum as well as a pub and says her motto is "If you can't help someone, don't hurt them."

Hennebury, also spelled Henneberry, is a long-established name in Quidi Vidi. The census for 1794 lists one of the inhabitants of the village as James Henneberry, a carpenter.

In 1936, names of residents of Quidi Vidi village listed in the Newfoundland Directory include: Henneberry, Mallard, Pynn, Snow, Bragg, Butler, Critch, Martin, Dawe, Squires, Murphy, O'Brien, Steele, Ring, Stone, Maher, Young, Morris, Emerson, Miller, Mayo and Scott.

# W. Lacey Amy

Someone who visited Newfoundland in 1870 wrote in Scribner's Monthly magazine that it was interesting when walking "in the suburbs of St. John's on a pleasant day to see the women and boys, who cure the fish while the men are gone to sea, driving carts into town from Quidiy Widy, Empty Basket and other little fishing ports drawn by diminutive ponies and laden with salt fish ready to be shipped to distant lands."

In 1882, Quidi Vidi had at least an acre of stages and flakes where cod fish was split, salted and dried. In August of 1882, the Evening Mercury had an update on the fishing season in Quidi Vidi and mentioned residents Messrs. Snow and Mallard, as well as a Mr. Skiffington. It was noted that Mr. Snow had lately purchased a fine cod trap from Mr. Vinnicombe which was almost new, having been in the water only half a dozen times.

*The cod traps operated out of Quidi Vidi were taken up the past week. The work done with them is very satisfactory. Mr. Snow's trap, for instance, netted from between 450 to 500 quintals (112 pounds equals one quintal), a fare which though large for so short a season and so small a number of hands was nevertheless surpassed last year by the same planter, whose take during the same season amounted to 650 quintals. Messrs. Skiffington and Mallard, also of Quidi Vidi, also have done well with their two traps, both of them hauling for over 300 quintals each. All three traps had been set in a miniature inlet a little north of Quidi Vidi, known as Robin Hood's Bay. It is formed of the bend of the coast, between Small Point and Sugar Loaf Head, and is something over a mile wide.*

By 1884, three merchants were living in Quidi Vidi, but the main occupation of inhabitants continued to be fishing, with 38 individuals engaged in catching and curing codfish. In 1891, 31 men were involved in catching and making fish and 17 women were also making fish. In Newfoundland, the process of salting and drying codfish on raised wooden platforms or flakes is referred to as "making fish."

The Census for the years 1884 and 1891 give an indication of the level of literacy in Quidi Vidi.

In 1884, 59 of the total population of 153 could read and write. By 1891, when the population had increased to 187, there were 97 people in Quidi Vidi who could read, and 67 of these individuals could also write. In 1884, 33 children were attending school and 26 were not. In 1891, 38 children under 15 had been to school the previous year and 50 of this age had not.

Picture Quidi Vidi on a summer day back in those early days. Cows, sheep, goats and hens wandering along the narrow, winding roads. The houses are close together, some have a flower garden and lilac or rose bushes. Near the houses there is likely a vegetable garden to grow potatoes, carrots, turnips, cabbages and beets, a weathered barn, and a summer supply of firewood stacked and ready for the winter. Stages and flakes rim the harbour.

In an article in the January 1912 issue of Canadian Magazine, writer W. Lacey Amy wrote about his trip to Newfoundland and how he had intended to avoid Quidi Vidi because, after hearing so much about it, he had concluded it was a tourist trap or, as he put it, a show fishing village.

*After it had headed the list of St. John's attractions of every Newfoundlander I talked to during the first day of my trip across the island, I changed the wording of my inquiry and asked for things worth seeing around St. John's – apart from Quidi Vidi, I mean.*

*But still each one persisted in commending his list with the fishing village, until I firmly made up my mind that if there was one spot in Newfoundland that I did not want to see it was this show place that I knew would have a high iron fence around it and a sign, "Don't point your umbrella at the picture."*

Determined not to visit Quidi Vidi, Amy ended up there by accident on the day of the annual regatta held at Quidi Vidi Lake, a stone's throw from the village. On the day of the regatta he walked up Signal Hill, leaving the crowds behind. Atop the hill he walked and walked until,

*Here opened far down in front a rickety cluster of houses, with a glimpse of glistening water and cod flakes. I had no idea it was Quidi Vidi; but what I did know was that there lay something I must see more closely, and for miles I clambered down the steep rocks along the water's edge.*

*Once I sank out of sight of the village and came upon the cable office, a break in the desertion, a little long, white building that concealed the conversational access to ocean-distant lands. There was no evidence that I was coming in touch with a guide-book route; the road I passed along was but a crude break in the rockiness, a byway making it easier for the foot-farer without mutilating the landscape.*

*The village had disappeared over a rugged rise, but I pushed on, with the knowledge that it would break upon me without disappointment.*

*Ahead of me the road branched into two forks and, following the*

*rougher, I came to the top of the rise, where the village came suddenly into sight, only a couple of hundred feet below me, the tall, rocky hillside arising abruptly behind it, and the ramshackle fish-houses hanging sleepily over the merest bit of glassy water.*

When Amy arrived in the village a passing fisherman told him he was in Quidi Vidi.

From Scribners Monthly, 1880

*I had come where I had intended not to; the mountain path had hoodwinked me into a spot I had wished to avoid. But there was no chiding of the deceiver — just a wonder that at last I had come upon the one great exception, and an admiration for the village that was, after all, no show village, but a real centre of a real industry that had unintentionally fashioned itself to suit the guide-book and the tourist, the lover of the quaint and the beautiful, but went along its way indifferent to its fame.*

*Down the roadway where vehicles had never passed, but where the village cattle or goats had worn a path deep into the grass, I passed. On one side a barbed-wire fence cut off not a detail of the view. On the other side a steep bank had been cut away when sometime it had been intended that this should be a real highway. The scene was like a painting, so quiet and lifeless was it. From where I stood there was no sign of movement save in the gentle, sun-touched ripple that sometimes fled across the bit of water, and a line of white clothes that waved lazily in the light breeze. The cod flakes were white with desertion where the cod lay baking, and dusty-dark where the owner had decided the sun was too warm for perfect drying. Not a sound came up to me to fit in with the anchored boats, the evidences of industry — nothing save the occasional bleat of an invisible goat. The few houses which made up the hamlet were splashed around on the rock with utter disregard for everything save a white road that ran along one side in irregular curves and twists, stamping itself by its colour as the belt-line route around the pond a mile away, on which the regatta sports were being held.*

Walking along a road which passed beneath cod flakes raised high on a network of long, spindly poles, Amy came finally to the edge of the village.

42

*Near the edge of the village a small stream had worn its way down through centuries until it boasted a gorge entirely out of proportion with the volume of water. And beside the hill-enclosed pond it fell into a shower of falls that gave the finishing touch to the native beauty of the spot. A few goats struggled for existence on the sparse verdure, placed there, it would seem, more for their picture-effect than for their own use.*

*Of course, now that I was in Quidi Vidi, I had to visit the spot from which all the local photographs are taken. To the top of the rock a well-worn path showed the reason for the advice I had received from admirers of Quidi Vidi, who saw I carried a camera. Everyone took pictures from that point. Acquiescing to conventions, I did the same. Below lay the village church, with its squatty steeple, the sole attempt at conventional architecture in the village. Close beside it was the tiny school, a building with ambitions, but limited realization. Its brown sides stood out abruptly fresh in colouring; in its short length an attempt had been made to squeeze in three windows, with the result that they crowded the end-wall with terrifying effect.*

*Climbing down the hill to the road the village ended abruptly in the gravelled, much-travelled highway that vindicated the guidebooks. Now it was a procession of cabs and carriages and automobiles filled with tourists and residents who had selected the long way around through Quidi Vidi to the regatta pond.*

*The show fishing village had ceased to be as suddenly as it had come into view. But it should always be. If anything in Newfoundland has justified itself in the list of local attractions, or to the traveller who sees it accidentally, Quidi Vidi can claim that distinction.*

In the City of St. John's Directory for 1915, residents of Quidi Vidi include 13 Mallard families, among them Thomas, a planter; fishermen Frank, Edward, John and Patrick; and Susie, a washerwoman. Ellen Mallard and Richard Mallard each had a house in Quidi Vidi and Bride Mallard, a clerk at Cross and Company, was boarding on Queen's Road. James Ring, a labourer, was living in the village in 1915 as were Arthur Bragg, a coachman and fishermen James and Stephen Bragg.

The resident Henneburys included fishermen Joseph, Thomas and William. Among the Horwoods were Jacob, a farmer; William, a fisherman; and John, a truckman. Also residing in Quidi Vidi were Mabel Snow, a nurse; Annie Snow, a dressmaker; Arthur Snow, a fisherman; Edgar Snow, a factory hand, and Hilda May Snow, an employee of the Imperial Tobacco Company.

# Queen Victoria Ross

Quidi Vidi escaped the fires which ravaged St. John's in 1817, 1818, 1846 and, the most devastating one of all, the 1892 fire which left almost 11,000 people homeless.

At the end of the 1892 fire, which began on a hot, windy July 8, more than three-quarters of the city of St. John's lay in ruins, and $20 million worth of property, including 2,000 houses and stores, had been destroyed. Following the fire, tents were set up near Quidi Vidi Lake for the homeless.

Quidi Vidi village escaped the Great Fires, but it is likely residents were affected by the Bank Crash that occurred in 1894. At that time Newfoundland had two banks in addition to the government Savings Bank. When one of the banks had to close its doors because of some reckless transactions, there was a run on the other two, both of which had to close. Banknotes immediately became valueless, business was brought to a standstill and workers were dismissed in large numbers. In one way or another the Bank Crash affected the whole population; large businesses went bankrupt and thrifty fishermen lost the savings they had acquired during a lifetime.

At the time of the Great Fire of 1892 a little girl named Queen Victoria Ross was living with her parents at Grove Farm, Quidi Vidi. The Winter 1996 issue of Newfoundland Ancestor carried an article written by grown-up Queen Victoria Ross-Young, in which she recalled the fire.

She began by saying she was named after Great Britain's Queen Victoria and was born March 23, 1885, in an old farmhouse at a place called Grove Farm, Quidi Vidi Road, north side. The farm was comprised of 100 acres and had an old rambling farmhouse that was perfect for her and her seven sisters.

On the day of the Great Fire of 1892, Queen was seven years old and visiting her eldest sister who had married a farmer named Thomas Martin and lived in the White Hills. When Queen saw clouds of smoke rising from the nearby city of St. John's she was so frightened that she ran home to Grove Farm.

She recalled that nearby fields soon began filling with those left homeless by the fire.

Queen's people came to Newfoundland from Nova Scotia. Her father had a shop on Water Street. He brought cattle and produce from Nova Scotia and Prince Edward Island, as well as 30-pound tubs of butter. He raised pigs and grew cabbages, turnips, potatoes and hay which he sold to the people of St. John's. Every day he provided the General Hospital with milk.

Her mother supplied Government House with milk, eggs, chicken, cream and fresh butter, and Queen fondly recalled going to the governor's mansion by horse and buggy and the cook inviting her into the kitchen for cake.

Mount Cashel, formerly the family home and property of the Howley family, was a combination residence and industrial training place for orphaned boys that was two miles away from Grove Farm. The orphanage was under the operation of Irish

Quidi Vidi village, c. 1890

Christian Brothers, the head in Queen's day was Brother Slattery, and her mother regularly walked there to teach the boys how to weave.

"Balley Haley" — now a golf course — was a farm that was home to an English officer, his wife and two daughters. After they left, Queen's father rented the property and raised vegetables.

She and her sisters were told the farmhouse on Grove Farm was part of a larger grander house that had burnt down. They were told great balls had been held at the large house. It was said French soldiers had once been stationed there and that was why there were secret dark closets and a large concealed apartment called The Hole. The house was rumoured to be haunted by a man who had been murdered there.

Queen wrote of Regatta Day, the Day of the Races, when the banks of Quidi Vidi Lake were transformed by the addition of dancing platforms and wheels of fortune and a greasy pole was floated out a number of feet into the water. The pole was heavily greased and contestants who successfully walked the full length were awarded a barrel of flour, 196 pounds of the ground grain in a wooden barrel.

Her father sold beer at the Regatta and her mother served lunches. Queen particularly remembered the day she helped her mother serve lunches and received a $1 tip. The lunch that day consisted of roast of spring lamb, new turnips and cabbages from Grove Farm, salt pork, fresh cream from the farm, as well as fresh strawberries and homemade cookies.

# The Regatta

*T*he Royal St. John's Regatta — Queen Elizabeth II approved use of the prefix "royal" in 1993 — is considered the oldest continuing sports event in North America and is traditionally held the first Wednesday in August on Quidi Vidi Lake. If the weather doesn't co-operate, the regatta is put off until the next suitable day. Since Regatta Day is both a municipal and provincial holiday in the Metropolitan St. John's area, the decision to go ahead or postpone is always a matter of great public interest.

On Regatta Day, booths and concessions operated by athletic, church and fraternal organizations, as well as by enterprising individuals, blanket the shoreline of Quidi Vidi Lake. The regatta is extremely popular, attracting up to 40,000 people annually.

According to John O'Mara, archivist for the regatta committee, the earliest known record of a rowing match in St. John's appeared in the Royal Gazette and Newfoundland Advertiser, August 6, 1816:

> *We understand a Rowing Match will take place on Monday Next between two boats upon which considerable bets are depending – they are to start at half past one o'clock, from alongside the prison ship.*

The first organized regatta was held on Tuesday, September 22, 1818, to mark the 47th anniversary of the coronation of King George III. Six boats participated and the Custom House boat won the silver cup.

Two days after the event, on September 24, the Mercantile Journal reported:

> *Tuesday last being the anniversary of our Beloved Sovereign it was celebrated by a display of colours etc. and about 2 o'clock the boats entered for the rowing match, advertised in the Sentinel of Saturday last, started six in number – the Silver Cup was won by the Custom House boat in 25 minutes, a distance of about two miles. The day was remarkably fine, a great number of boats attended the race which rendered the scene particularly interesting.*

Historian Paul O'Neill says the mention of two miles would seem to indicate the regatta was held in St. John's Harbour and not on Quidi Vidi Lake.

The regatta had moved to its present location on Quidi Vidi Lake by 1829. The Royal Gazette informed its readers: "Thursday is the day appointed for the rowing matches on Quidi Vidi Lake and

Saturday for the sailing matches on the harbour."

Governor Thomas Cochrane — who arrived in Newfoundland in 1825 to take up his duties as the colony's first civilian governor and completed construction of Government House in 1831— lent his patronage to the 1829 races, the last year there are records of races being held in St. John's Harbour. A second regatta, however, was held in the harbour on August 19, 1845, in honour of the visit of Prince Henry of the Netherlands.

The year 1853 saw a three-day regatta, the longest in the event's history.

In 1855, a crew of Quidi Vidi fishermen rowed in the Lady Darling and defeated a crew from St. John's in the Undine in a challenge race. The prize was £50 and, after the race, the owner of the boat made a present of it to the winning crew.

The first women's race on record was rowed in 1856 and was won by a crew from Quidi Vidi who defeated a crew from the Battery. The names of the winning crew were: Ellen Walsh, stroke; Jennie King, Mary Brace, Lizzie Hauton, Crissie Squires and Jessie Needham. Robert Hennebury was coxswain.

The Prince of Wales (later Edward VII) was a guest at the 1860 regatta and offered a prize of £100 to the winners of the Fisherman's Race. The prince not only attended the regatta, he delighted residents of Quidi Vidi by going there to examine the fishing stages and chat to fishermen and their wives.

After 1860 there was no regatta for 11 years. Following the revival of the regatta in 1871, some of the boats weighed as much as 800 pounds. Between 1873 and 1915, fishermen from Outer Cove had the fastest time of the day in 16 of those years.

In 1877, the Prince of Wales prize was won by a crew of fishermen from Placentia rowing in a boat called the Placentia. The boat was built by Edward Sinnott and rowed by five Morrisseys and a Whalen who were all more than six feet tall. The story is that the so-called Placentia Giants walked to and from St. John's, carrying their boat on their shoulders.

Outer Cove won five consecutive championships from 1883 to 1887. In 1885, they won the Fisherman's Race in the Myrtle in a record time of nine minutes 20 seconds which lasted for 16 years.

The regatta of 1892 was cancelled because the shores of Quidi Vidi Lake were lined with tents to house those left homeless by the Great Fire of July 8.

The first modern racing shells were introduced to the regatta in the 1890s. Most of these six-man, fixed-seat boats were built by Robert Sexton, a St. John's carriage maker who constructed racing shells as a sideline. The Glencoe was the first of these shells, but the most famous was the Blue Peter.

In 1901, a team from Torbay in the Red Cross, a boat built by Robert Sexton, raced against a team from Outer Cove in the Blue Peter. The Outer Cove team, consisting of Walter Power, coxswain;

**Under the flakes of Quidi Vidi**

John Whelan, stroke; Daniel McCarthy, Denis McCarthy, Dennis Croke, Martin Boland and John Nugent won in a record breaking time of 9:13.8.

The Lord Warden of Scotland, a visitor to the Regatta in 1910, offered seven gold medals to be awarded to the crew who could beat the 1901 time. The Outer Cove record stood, however, for 80 years, until it was broken in 1981 by the Smith Stockley team, who brought in the Native in a time of 9:12.4.

Cox for the Smith Stockley team was Jim Ring of Quidi Vidi. The team was made of his sons, Randy, stroke, and Paul, as well as Brian Cranford, Bill Holwell, John Barrington, and Tom Power.

In 1919, a Victory Regatta was held to celebrate the end of the First World War. The Prince of Wales (later King Edward VIII) was in attendance. The regatta was marred by the drowning of Sgt. Charlie Peters when the Nellie R sank. The Coronation Regatta of 1937 marked the crowning of King George VI. That year, the races were broadcast on radio for the first time by the Dominion Broadcasting Company. No regatta was held in 1940 due to the outbreak of the Second World War.

The regatta of 1945 was dubbed the Victory Regatta to celebrate the end of the war. In 1949, the Ladies' Races were revived. Gert Reardigan became the first female coxswain in 1977. In 1999, women rowed in 20 of 29 races and there were 88 women's crews, compared to 34 men's crews.

In 1982, the Outer Cove men's crew, rowing in the Blue Peter 4, set a new course record of 9:03.48. In 1991, Smith Stockley/Outer Cove men's crew broke the nine-minute barrier and set a new course record of 8:59.42 in the Men's Championship Race.

Almost 90 years earlier, Regatta Day 1893, the shores of Quidi Vidi Lake were graced by the presence of a wondrous oriental palace. According to writer Jack Fitzgerald, Professor Charles Danielle opened a splendid structure at the head of Quidi Vidi Lake which was dubbed the Royal Lake Pavilion. It was described in The Evening Telegram as "a magnificent oriental palace open to the genteel and responsible public on Regatta Day and every day where everything obtainable at the best hotels on this side of the world will be served by young ladies and gentlemen attendants attired in oriental costumes."

The paper said "hot (red hot!) meals" would be served in the ballroom, which was large enough to accommodate 1,500 guests, while the banquet hall would be reserved for serving dainty refreshments. In 1895, the eccentric professor tore down the pavilion and used the wood to construct his famous Octagon Castle at Octagon Pond. Danielle died in May 1902 and was buried in the Anglican cemetery on Forest Road in a casket he designed and built and had earlier put on public display at Octagon Castle.

The regatta was not the only competition the lake hosted.

In 1812, a mock battle was fought on frozen Quidi Vidi Lake to keep up the morale of soldiers stationed in St. John's. There was a sleigh race on the lake in 1821 featuring two ponies, White Foot and Black Dwarf. The winner is unknown. Curling matches took place on the lake before the construction of the Avalon Curling and Skating Rink in 1870.

O'Neill says in February 1896, ice was cleared on Quidi Vidi Lake for a game of hockey played with inverted walking sticks and a cricket ball. Just before the turn of the century a cricket pitch was constructed on the north shore of Quidi Vidi Lake. At the turn of the century, the first municipal swimming pools were built on the south shore of Quidi Vidi Lake and at Long Pond.

The novelty at the 1906 regatta was a swimming race across Quidi Vidi Lake, won by E.J. Birch. This event was continued up to 1914 when the First World War put a halt to the regatta because most of the oarsmen were overseas fighting.

The grounds near Quidi Vidi Lake were called Pleasantville and they were a popular spot for picnickers. In September 1914 a military camp was established at Pleasantville. The first 500 volunteers in the Newfoundland Regiment, the famous First Five Hundred, men known as Blue Puttees because of the colour of their leg wrappings, were in training at Pleasantville until October 3, 1914. On that day they marched to Water Street and boarded the SS Florizel, headed across the ocean to help Great Britain fight and win the First World War.

# Fort Pepperrell

*T*he First World War lasted from 1914 to 1918. It was called the Great War and the War to end all Wars, but 21 years later, in 1939, most of the world was plunged into yet another global conflict.

**Sir William Pepperrell**

In 1941, not long after the beginning of the Second World War, the British government signed an agreement with the United States which included the granting of military bases in Newfoundland and Labrador for a period of 99 years. On January 25, 1941, the Edmund B. Alexander arrived in St. John's with 1,000 American troops on board, the first Americans to serve on foreign soil in the Second World War.

Base construction began at Pleasantville, near Quidi Vidi, on May 5, 1941.

The new installation — designed by Lieutenant-Colonel Philip Burton, an urban planner from Texas, in the shape of a 10-gallon Stetson hat — was to be called Fort Pepperrell, after Sir William Pepperrell, the soldier who led the American colonists in the capture of the fortress of Louisburg in 1745 and was also a distant relative of the Outerbridge family of St. John's.

The initial plan and design for the military base called for accommodation for a garrison of 3,500 troops, but the military increased this figure to 5,500 early in 1942. The duties of the garrison included the defense of United States bases in Argentia and Stephenville, as well as St. John's harbour and the airfield at nearby Torbay.

Because their new accommodations were not yet ready, the Americans arriving in Newfoundland stayed on board the Alexander until May 1941, when a temporary camp was erected for approximately 1,000 troops.

On April 15, a lease had been signed with Carpasian Park Limited for 15 acres of land at the southwest corner of Carpasian and Long Pond roads on which to erect a temporary land base. Camp Alexander, as it became known, was occupied on May 20 as work continued on Fort Pepperrell, where the barracks were two-storey, flat-roof structures, wood framed with asbestos shingles.

On November 24 the move from Camp Alexander was begun, and in February 1942 Headquarters was moved from Sir Richard Squires' old house at 44 Rennie's Mill Road, where it had been set up a year before.

Coming close on the heels of the Depression, the building of Fort Pepperrell and the jobs made available to civilians were a great economic boost for Newfoundland, but the Americans made other contributions as well.

In 1941, they realized they would need a dock with maximum military security, so the United States Government acquired the shoreline of the Battery, at the northeastern end of St. John's harbour, and the first "modern" pier in the port was built just east of Temperance Street to supply Fort Pepperrell. The dock remained in the possession of the United States until 1961, when it reverted to Canadian ownership and was operated by the National Harbours Board of Canada.

The base also operated radio station VOUS, which carried all the best U.S. radio-network shows and Armed Forces Radio Service broadcasts.

Over the course of the Second World War, 25,000 Newfoundland girls married American servicemen and moved to the United States, a mass exodus of about 10 per cent of the total population. When the war ended in 1945, Fort Pepperrell was transferred from the U.S. Army to the U.S. Air Force. On April 14, 1958, it was announced that the base would be phased out and all civilians would be dismissed from their jobs by the year's end.

On May 17, 1958, thousands of citizens turned out for the final Armed Forces Day celebrations and finally, on May 15, 1960, the last American forces departed when the United States Army Transportation Terminal Command Arctic closed its headquarters.

On August 10, 1961, the property was formally returned to Newfoundland, the American flag was lowered and the Union Jack and the Canadian Red Ensign raised. Canadian military headquarters was transferred from Buckmaster's Field to the former American headquarters. In 1966, the base hospital, which had been turned over to the Newfoundland Government, was reopened as a hospital for sick children. The Dr. Charles A. Janeway Hospital was named for the Boston doctor who had advised that such a centre be set up. The hospital was in operation up until May 2001, when a newly built Janeway opened off Prince Philip Parkway.

When the Americans left, the name Fort Pepperrell was dropped and the former American base reverted to the name Pleasantville. The structures left behind became federal and provincial government offices, apartment buildings operated by the Newfoundland Government, and storage units occupied by various government agencies.

# The Rings of Quidi Vidi

*I*f there is any one family whose name is synonymous with the annual regatta on Quidi Vidi Lake it is the Rings of Quidi Vidi village. The matriarch of the family is Kathleen, who lives in the village in a brown brick house with a front door featuring brown-robed St. Francis of Assisi feeding forest animals. A wooden plaque next to the door says this is the home of James Ring senior and Kathleen. The Rings began building their house in 1934. Quidi Vidi Lake, where the regatta takes place every August, is over the hill behind their house.

The Rings are long-time residents of Quidi Vidi whose association with the regatta goes back years. Kathleen takes pride in saying that her husband, Jim, who died of a heart attack in 1987 at age 75, was a coxswain in the regatta for 59 years and first got involved in the boat races in the 1920s. In 1981, he was cox of the Smith Stockley men's crew who made regatta history by edging out the 9:13.8 record of 1901 with a time of 9:12:04. Jim's sons, Paul and Randy, were members of the winning team.

A plaque with the record-breaking time etched on it hangs on the fireplace in the living room. Kathleen says the 1981 win left her husband

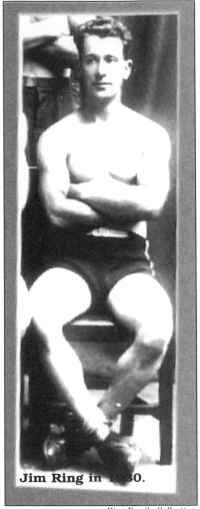

Jim Ring in 1930.

Ring Family Collection

with mixed emotions. He was happy with the victory, but taking the 80-year-old record away from Outer Cove gave him pangs of conscience.

Kathleen herself, who was born on June 7, 1915, rowed in one race on Quidi Vidi Lake. That was back in August 1930 and she was a member of a women's crew who won the St. Joseph's Regatta organized by Father Pippy, the priest at St. Joseph's Roman Catholic church. A picture of the team hangs on the wall of the small room off the front door that she calls her rowing room. Besides Kathleen, the team, including one spare, consisted of Susan Mallard, Hanna Hennebury, Queen May, Margaret Morris,

Dolly Byrne and Margaret Bragg. Cox was Art Snow.

In another picture frame there are two photographs: one is of Kathleen, aged 15, and looking very grown up in a v-necked, sleeveless dress and strap shoes; the other is of Jim, aged 18, bare-chested and wearing his rowing shorts.

Nearby is the framed letter of congratulations Queen Elizabeth II sent Jim and his crew in 1981. The queen wrote: "As Head Warden of the Cinque Ports I am most interested to learn that, at the St. John's Regatta in August of this year, the Smith Stockley crew lowered the record for the course previously established by the Outer Cove crew in 1901, and are to be presented with the Lord Warden's medal."

That medal, kept with others the family has won over the years, says on one side Lord Warden's Prize 1910, and on the other 1981 Regatta won by Jim Ring senior, cox, 9:12.04.

Jim and Kathleen were childhood sweethearts who grew up in Quidi Vidi village. His parents were blacksmith Jim Ring and his wife Elizabeth (Snow), who lived in a house near the Catholic school.

Kathleen's parents were John Maher, who went to sea for 45 years,

Ring Family Collection

**Kathleen Ring at 15 (above) and today (inset)**

and his wife, Mary (Bragg), known as Queenie. Kathleen was raised with nine brothers and sisters in a house now occupied by her son, Paul.

Kathleen Maher married Jim Ring at St. Joseph's Church on February 26, 1933. Jim worked as a fisherman and stonemason and he and Kathleen raised a family of 10 children, eight still living in Quidi Vidi. All of the Rings — Jimmy, Jack, Claude, Paul, Lottie, Elaine, Betty, Carmelita, Madonna and Randy — have rowed in the regatta at one time or other, and grandchildren and great-grandchildren are continuing the family tradition. In 2002, Jim and Kathleen's granddaughter, Bernadine, marked her 20th year of rowing in the regatta.

**The St. John's Regetta, as depicted by the Canadian Illustrated News, September 4, 1875.**

**Some of the Ring family's Regatta medals.**

# Aviation on Quidi Vidi

As well as being the site of annual boat races, Quidi Vidi Lake also has an impressive aviation history. On May 15, 1910, the U.S. Navy Airship C-5 commanded by Lieutenant Commander Emory Coil, left Montau, New York, and navigated a distance of 1,945 kilometres to a former cricket field in Pleasantville in a record time of 25 hours and 50 minutes.

The next evening a radio telegraph signal reported the airship had broken adrift from moorings at Pleasantville. There were no casualties but 10 individuals were given instructions to bring down the airship with anti-aircraft fire. The craft, which measured 192 feet long, was last seen near Trepassey moving just above icebergs as it blew out to sea, apparently out of control.

In February 1919, Major Farifax Morgan came to Newfoundland to search for a level field at least 100 yards long to use as an aircraft runway, and found Pleasantville on the shores of Quidi Vidi Lake.

At that time, The Daily Mail was offering a prize for the first non-stop transatlantic flight and Morgan was anxious to get an edge on his competitors. However, by the time he and his partner, F. Raynham, arrived on April 10 with their crew and equipment, former RAF ace Harry Hawker and Lieutenant Mackenzie Grieve were already preparing for an attempt to fly the Atlantic from Glendenning meadow at Mount Pearl.

On May 18, 1919, both crews decided to try a transatlantic flight.

Raynham and Morgan attempted a flight from their field at Quidi Vidi but their plane crashed on take-off, severely injuring Morgan who never flew again. Due to an overheated radiator, Hawker and Mackenzie were forced to land their plane in the Atlantic where they were rescued by a Danish tramp steamer. Even though the Mackenzie/Grieve attempt ended in disaster, the two pilots had the distinction of making the first airplane flight in Newfoundland on April 10, 1919.

The winner of the Daily Mail prize was the team of John Alcock and Arthur Whitten Brown who took off from Lester's Field in St. John's on June 14, 1919, and arrived at Clifden in Galway, Ireland, 16 hours and 57 minutes later.

In the 1920s there was a hangar on the boathouse site, put there by an Australian airman named Captain Sidney Cotton who had flown with the Royal Flying Corps in the First World War. Cotton arrived in Newfoundland in 1921. The next year, he started an aviation enterprise called the Aerial Survey Company (Newfoundland) Limited with Lieutenant David Plaistowe, another war veteran, and Captain Sydney Bennett, a Newfoundland pilot. Although they managed to have three airplanes in service at one time, by 1923 their attempt to establish a local airline was deemed a failure and

abandoned.

In 1930, Newfoundlanders Captain Douglas Fraser and Arthur Sullivan, flying partners in Sullivan's company, Newfoundland Airways Limited, landed a contract to airlift mail to and from Newfoundland ports of call during the winter. Their base of operation was in a hangar on the north bank of Quidi Vidi Lake, just west of the mouth of Virginia River. In 1931, the partnership was over and Fraser used the site as headquarters for his own company, Old Colony Airways. On July 12, 1933, Fraser was busy at the hangar when he saw a plane land on the water of the lake. Much to his amazement, he saw that the occupants of the aircraft were famed aviator Charles Lindbergh and his wife, Anne. A year earlier the kidnapping and murder of the Lindbergh's toddler son had horrified the world. A German-born carpenter, Bruno Hauptmann, was later found guilty of the crime and executed.

On May 20, 1927, Lindbergh had flown over Newfoundland during his historic non-stop flight from New York to Paris. On this trip, part of a 30,000-mile survey that was to help in establishing base sites for future air routes, the Lindberghs had lost their way trying to find Bay Bulls Big Pond, where a reception and hundreds of citizens were waiting to greet them. Fraser rowed out to the plane and gave instructions which the Lindberghs used to land successfully on Bay Bulls Big Pond. On January 11, 1938, Captain Douglas Fraser landed his single engine Fox Moth in Gander, making the first official landing at what became known as the Newfoundland Airport.

# Allan Bragg

By Peter Stacey

*A*llan Bragg was born in Quidi Vidi in 1921 and has never thought of leaving. His house, on Cuckhold's Cove Road, is modern. He says it was constructed over and around the double house where he grew up. His father, Jim, and his uncle Stephen built the double house for themselves and their families. Allan's grandfather, Stephen Bragg, used to have a house next door to his sons, beside Quidi Vidi Battery.

His grandfather, son of a man who came to Quidi Vidi from Bonavista Bay, was born and raised in Quidi Vidi and married Mathilda Whalen from Grates Cove, Conception Bay. Both of Allan's parents grew up in Quidi Vidi, his father in the house by the Battery, his mother, Christine (Maher), in a house not far from Christ Church.

In Allan's living room there is a black-and-white photograph showing his grandfather sitting and his grandmother standing next to him with one hand on his shoulder. There is a picture of Allan's parents, and one of his father as a dashing young man wearing a bow tie and a salt-and-pepper hat.

On the walls in the living room and front porch there are photographs of Quidi Vidi in the 1800s and wonderful shots of residents making fish. On the wall in the living room there's a colourful painting Allan was given as a gift. The artist said it was of Quidi Vidi, but Allan knows it isn't.

There are photographs of Allan's brothers and sisters, Maud, Florence, Margaret, Jim, Edward, Jack and Bill. There are pictures as well of Allan and his wife before and after their marriage. Allan married Ruby Barnes from Signal Hill Road in 1946. She passed away in 1998.

Allan and Ruby had five children, one of whom died in infancy. Coloured photographs of children and grandchildren stretch out along the walls next to black-and-white likenesses of long dead relatives. There are two photographs of Allan as a good-looking young man, very like his father. In both pictures, the hills of Quidi Vidi are behind him and the sea is visible.

Allan's house sits feet away from cliffs which overlook the harbour and the ocean just beyond the Gut.

From his living room window, he can look down at the Gut, the waters wild and angry on a windy winter's day, deceptively gentle and calm on a still day in summer. Allan talks of an uncle he never knew who drowned in the Gut one summer's day. The uncle, then a boy of 12, was returning home with his father after a day of fishing when the winds came up and the Gut suddenly became a place of pounding, treacherous, deadly waves. The boy's father put him off on rocks in what seemed a sheltered spot, but a wave came and swept him to his death.

In 1936, when Allan was 15, there were 42 households in Quidi Vidi and two schools. From his window, Allan can see where the schools he remembers once stood. St. Thomas, the Anglican school, was not far from Christ Church, St. Joseph's, the Catholic school, was on a hill overlooking the church. Allan attended St. Joseph's, no more than a five-minute walk down over the hill from his house. His teacher was Miss Leamon from St. John's. The teacher at St. Thomas was a young woman from Bonavista Bay who boarded with the Emerson family in Quidi Vidi during the school year.

Allan ruefully admits he wasn't an ideal student. He recalls skipping classes to go catch rabbits in the hills around Quidi Vidi, with his catechism and his Royal reader tucked away in his back pocket for safekeeping.

When he finished with school Allan did whatever he could to earn a living. He went fishing like his father, he worked at the Newfoundland Brewery in St. John's, he did plastering work with the Conway family. During the Second World War, he became a member of the Newfoundland Regiment and was stationed on Bell Island. The war brought Allan one trip across the water to Canada — "that was overseas," he grins.

In 1941, he traveled to Halifax on the ferry Caribou as one of the escorts for German prisoners of war who had been captured in the waters off Newfoundland and brought to St. John's. The first part of the trip was by train across the island from St. John's to Port aux Basques.

The next leg was on the ferry and the trip across the Gulf was so rough that one of the German prisoners rolled out of his bunk and onto the floor of the cabin.

A year after Allan's voyage on the Caribou, on October 14, 1942, the vessel was attacked by a German submarine while carrying 238 passengers and crew across the Gulf. The 101 survivors were rescued by the Royal Canadian Navy.

# Fish Plants, Breweries and Restaurants

*I*n the years after the war, when two fish plants were built in Quidi Vidi, Allan was among residents of the community who found work there.

The house where Allan lives is on Cuckhold's Cove Road, just past Cuckhold's Cove. According to the Encyclopedia of Newfoundland and Labrador, M.F. Howley (1901) says the name Cuckhold's Cove originates from the fish which were commonly caught in the area. The species of fish known as bream is similar to a southern ocean species, the cuckhold (Ostracion camellinus), hence the name Cuckhold's Cove. In 1796 a detachment of the Royal Newfoundland Regiment was stationed at Cuckhold Head to repel a French fleet approaching St. John's.

The Illustrated Tribune (1909) notes the landing of submarine cables at Cuckhold's Cove in 1909. In 1931 the Commercial Cable Company of New York operated a total of eight transatlantic cables connecting Waterville, Ireland, to Canso, Nova Scotia and Far Rockway, New York, by way of the Cuckhold's Cove cable station. M.O. Doxsee (1948) reported that these cables suffered damage as a result of the earthquake of 1929.

In 1939, in spite of government assistance and market demand, only a few Newfoundland companies, including Job Brothers and Company and Harvey's Limited, were involved in the fresh-frozen fish industry. That year Newfoundland produced 1.5 million pounds of frozen groundfish, but with the outbreak of the Second World War the fresh-frozen fish industry took off. Great Britain needed new sources of food to feed its own population and to support the war effort and looked to North America, including Newfoundland, for a supply of frozen fish.

By 1943 there were 14 freezing plants in operation. Production went from 12.6 million pounds of frozen fish in 1943 to 34.4 million pounds in 1945, when there were 18 freezing and 44 filleting plants in operation. When the war ended in 1945, British demand for fish fell off sharply and fish-plant operators concentrated on establishing a presence in U.S. markets.

In the late 1960s or early 1970s, as the Newfoundland fishery began to meet problems of competition from foreign "distant-water" fleets and declining catches attributable to stock depletion, most non-resident companies sold out or closed their operations. When further expansion began in the late 1970s, in anticipation of larger catches with the extension of Canada's fisheries jurisdiction to 200 nautical miles from the coast, three companies dominated, accounting for about 70 per cent of the total value of fish processed in the province by 1980.

The largest company was Fishery Products Limited, a firm which had been a key actor in the expansion of frozen-fish processing since the 1940s under the direction of Arthur and Denis Monroe. By 1980, the company operated its own trawler fleet, supplying plants with the capability to operate year-round at Burin, Marystown, Trepassey, Catalina and Harbour Breton, as well as several seasonal "inshore" and "feeder" plants.

The second firm was Lake Group Fisheries, a local family-operated concern, which had its roots in an export company founded by H.B.C. Lake in Fortune. That company expanded its interests in fish freezing under Lake's son, Spencer. The Lake Group was first established at Gaultois, Englee and Burgeo. In 1974, Lake made a bid to become one of the dominant firms in the business in 1974 by acquiring Bonavista Cold Storage, which operated major plants at Bonavista, Grand Bank and Fermeuse. The Lake Group took over Fortune Fisheries Limited in 1978 and was also connected with the firm of John Penney and Sons of Ramea up until 1981.

The third dominant company was Canada's largest fishing and fish-processing company, National Sea Products Limited, which established a corporate presence in this province in 1970 by purchasing the former Ross-Steers fish plant on the south side of St. John's Harbour.

The Lake Group bought some of their fish from Cabot Seafoods, a fish plant in Quidi Vidi which was owned and operated by Glen Bursey. It was later purchased by Harvey Best and renamed Village Seafoods. Now reconstructed, the former fish plant is the home of the Quidi Vidi Brewing Company. A place that's hard to miss, the brewery sits surrounded by granite cliffs at the mouth of the harbour to Quidi Vidi village.

With its green spruce clapboard and white trim, the building looks comfortably at home within the rustic surroundings of the village. Founded in 1996 by Newfoundland engineers Dave Rees and Dave Fong, the brewery is 100 per cent locally owned and operated. The ultra-modern facility houses a state of the art brewery, retail store, administrative offices and reception room. One of the things that sets the local brewery apart from national breweries is that the design and location of the plant are deeply connected to the local roots of its founders.

The Stagehead restaurant, located in front of the Quidi Vidi Brewery Company, sits on the site of yet another former fish plant. Fort Amherst Seafoods was established in 1945 by William Joseph Bursey and although the fish plant is no longer in existence, the property remains in the Bursey family.

W.J. Bursey was born in Old Perlican, Trinity Bay, in 1892, and by 1910 was operating a cod liver oil factory at Lead Cove, Trinity Bay. That same year he left Newfoundland and moved to the U.S. and Canada, where he worked as a labourer and machinist.

In 1916 he returned to Newfoundland and got back into the fishery business. In 1923, he purchased a small fish premise on the South Battery in St. John's and by 1924 had started a cod liver oil business which he expanded in 1932 when he rented and later purchased the fishing premises of James Guest on the Southside. One day in 1941, he had a visitor from the United States Armed Forces who asked if he would be willing to rent his Southside premises to moor the American troop ship Edmund B. Alexander. The ship that brought 1,500 American troops to St. John's remained tied up at Bursey's wharf for eight months.

In 1943, the Southside property was expropriated and Bursey bought premises on Duckworth Street near City Hall, where he had a store and a smoke house. He smoked kippers, salmon, cod fillets and capelin and by the spring of 1944 the smoke was bothering City Hall so much he was forced to move his smoke house.

He rented premises in Quidi Vidi from Mr. Pynn, a longtime resident, and put up a new building and two concrete smokers. In his autobiography, The Undaunted Pioneer, Bursey wrote that each smoker was 10 feet square and 25 feet high with a smoke-proof concrete partition. Each smoke house was therefore divided into two smoking chambers where 10,000 kippers could be smoked in one process. He sold smoked kippers, smoked cod fillets and smoked salmon to markets as far away as Bermuda and South Africa. W.J. Bursey died in 1980. His son, Ray, enlarged the fish plant in 1965.

By 1986 the fish plant was closed and the Burseys opened a restaurant called the Flakehouse on the site. That restaurant, which was in operation for about 10 years, has been replaced by the Stagehead, run by Ray Bursey, son of Ray and grandson of W.J.

Over the years, Quidi Vidi has mirrored Newfoundland and Labrador in the changes both have witnessed.

Offshore waters fished by migratory fishermen. Claimed by England. Sporadic settlement. Pirate attacks. Military attacks. Continuing settlement. Fluctuations in the fishery. Birth and death. War and peace. Collapse of the codfishery.

And now, looking towards a new future where tourism plays an important role, where the beauty and wildness that is Newfoundland and Labrador will be discovered and marvelled over by a new generation of those who come from away.

Quidi Vidi today.

By John Parker

---

## Stage Head

### Step back in Tyme

Banquet, Meeting & Catering Facilities

When choosing a location for your next business or private function, consider the Stage Head in historic Quidi Vidi Village. The Stage Head is architecturally fashioned after an early Newfoundland structure known as a fishing stage, which was primarily used as a fish processing and fishing gear storage facility. These buildings, located near the water, also served as cookhouses and provided shelter from the elements for the hardy fishermen. The Stage Head refers to that part of the stage which was adjacent to the water where the boats would be tied up. The present Stage Head, surrounded by the historic charm of Quidi Vidi Village, attempts to capture and preserve the flavour of this unique coastal heritage.

Stage Head Catering Services Ltd. can provide a variety of products and services that suit all your needs. We are courteous, energetic and always helpful when you want to provide that little extra something to ensure that your function is a complete success.

# Producer of a wide variety of exceptional food products.

www.purity.nf.ca

*Something for everyone!*

*Milk that makes your day!*

From the Collection of Peg Magnone

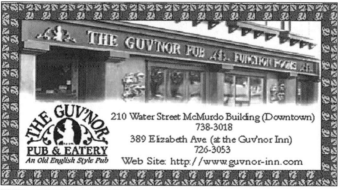

J ean Edwards Stacey is a
journalist in St. John's
and author of:
**Historic Homes of
Newfoundland**,
and
**Memoirs of a Blue Puttee:
The Newfoundland Regiment
in World War One**,
both published by DRC
Publishing, and also of
**Government House
Life and Times.**

Jean is currently at work on a number of new books,
including Historic Homes of Newfoundland and Labrador.
She lives in St. John's with her husband, Peter Stacey
and they have three children, David, Robyn and Christopher.